CW01213842

FREEDOM VILLAGE

FREEDOM VILLAGE

A MEMOIR

MARY ROSENBERGER

Payette Publishing LLC
110 W. 31st St., Ste. 202
Garden City, ID 83714
https://payettepublishing.com

© 2024 by Mary Rosenberger. All rights reserved. Please support authors and their creative expressions by respecting copyright laws. No portion of this book may be reproduced without explicit prior written permission.

This book represents a collection of the author's memories of her own lived experience inside and beyond the walls of Freedom Village USA. While the author has made every effort to ensure accuracy, neither author nor publisher assumes responsibility for errors or inconsistencies with others' lived experiences.

First edition.

ISBN 979-8-9909769-0-0 (hardcover); 979-8-9909769-1-7 (ebook)

Library of Congress Control Number: 2024916743

Cover art by Grayson Lawless.

Bible verses from THE HOLY BIBLE, NEW INTERNATIONAL VERSION®, NIV® Copyright © 1973, 1978, 1984, 2011 by Biblica, Inc.® Used by permission. All rights reserved worldwide.

To my mom and dad:
You laid pure faith as the foundation of our family. Your songs and stories filled me with wonder and belief. You planted truth deep in my heart. Life buried it in fear, but love remains and even grows despite fear and pain. Nothing is wasted.
This is for you.

CONTENTS

Introduction: How Long, Lord? 1

1. Freedom Village USA 11

2. Obedience Brings Blessings; Disobedience Brings
   Consequences 24

3. Salvation and Conviction 31

4. Descent 37

5. My So-Called Perfect Life 43

6. Darkness 51

7. Falling in Love 65

8. Hard Love 77

9. Kool-Aid 91

10. The Forbidden Thought 98

11. The Leaving 111

12. Out from the Inside 118

13. Aftershocks 125

14. Epiphany 130

15. Freedom 143

A Note from the Author 152

A Note from the Publisher 154

Book Club Questions 157

Resources for Readers 159

Acknowledgments 163

About the Author 167

CONTENT ADVISORY

This book addresses topics that might be disturbing to some people. These include spiritual abuse, mental abuse, poverty, suicidal ideation, self-harm, eating disorders, depression, anxiety, and postpartum depression and anxiety. Please take care of yourself and check in on your own emotions as you read *Freedom Village: A Memoir*.

Resources addressing these topics can be found at the end of the book.

INTRODUCTION
HOW LONG, LORD?

I STARTED my first real job when I was thirty years old, working at a café in the Finger Lakes region of New York. My coworkers and customers didn't know anything about me or my upbringing. I quickly realized that our pasts were fundamentally different. I was born into a life at Freedom Village USA—billed as a Christian home for troubled teens—where my parents worked for more than three decades. My coworkers found the stories I told about growing up in Freedom Village, becoming a staff member, and ultimately leaving it all behind at age twenty-four downright unbelievable. As I talked to people from the "outside" about what my life had been like on the "inside" of Freedom Village, it became clear that it was impossible to do justice to my story during busy café shifts. I decided to write my story and share it online for my new friends and acquaintances to read.

The idea to write my story deepened into such a desire that I'm not sure I could have avoided writing my blog, *Out from the Inside*, even if I had tried. The profoundly therapeutic results brought about by the process of writing about my life were unimaginable to me at the time.

I started writing my blog about my earliest years and slowly moved through my history the way I recalled it. I picked through a veritable dumpster of memories, seeking those that I thought defined my childhood at Freedom Village. What began as a desire merely to document my life story turned into something that actually changed my mind and saved my life. I didn't realize it at the time, but the writing process was the beginning of my healing process.

Still, I never expected my story to resonate the way it has with religious people outside of Freedom Village. Many who initially responded with ever-widening eyes and gasps of "Oh my gosh, that sounds like a cult!" would later read my blog and share a different, more personal response: "I really identify with your story."

For a while, I thought I must have been a magnet for people who have experienced oppressive religious systems. But I began to realize that spiritual abuse and fear-laced doctrines are alive and well in *so many* churches. People from numerous different Christian denominations have told me that they were taught the exact same lies about God as I was. Friends of mine who go to "Bible-believing, Bible-preaching churches" live in a similar culture of fear, paranoia, and control as I lived in at Freedom Village. My story is unique, but somehow, it's also common. I'm compelled to keep telling my story for those who see themselves in it—because I now know that hope exists.

These days, I am in an ever-growing state of healing and peace. My mind, once a place of chaos and confusion, is now clear and open. I am learning to embrace difficulty and pain with love, instead of avoiding them in fear. I've been deeply hurt, but I can look at those I once viewed as my enemies through a lens of love. I've experienced nothing short of a miracle.

When I wrote the blog over the course of 2018, I could only look at my past through the lens of fear. That was a large reason why I never stated the name Freedom Village in *Out from the Inside*: I was afraid of the repercussions that could come from my speaking out. I was afraid of the inevitable social media response that arises whenever Freedom Village is addressed. It seemed safer to keep everything anonymous. I told myself that it was the high road, the classier thing to do, the way to avoid conflict.

After all, my life at Freedom Village is a complex experience to process. The more I thought about it, the more questions resulted. Was it a cult, or was it a God-ordained ministry? Was it Heaven, or was it Hell?

As I began publicly telling my story, I discovered that either side of these oppositions did indeed seem to apply for those who lived within Freedom Village. Many called it a cult. Many called it the place that saved their lives. I angered both sides when I published new blog posts, and I began to feel the full truth of both realities. On the outside of Freedom Village, I discovered the beauty of *both/and*, when all I knew for twenty-four years was *either/or*.

I left Freedom Village in 2011, and afterward, someone shared a cult checklist with me—something like "20 Warning Signs of a Cult." Freedom Village checked every box. I laughed it off, unable yet to acknowledge that I had suffered abuse and brainwashing during my time there. But as I wrote posts for *Out from the Inside*, I began to see the culture of fear, the unquestioning obedience to authority, and the spiritual manipulation for what they were. I was becoming disillusioned with the life of "full-time Christian service" that I had lived; my family had been severely mistreated in God's name. Fury, shame, grief, and sorrow washed over me as I acknowledged that hard truth, making me regret ever saying anything good about Freedom Village. All of my good memories seemed ruined. I wanted to weep over the truth that I had been abused for so long, all the time believing it was love. I felt stupid. I felt used. I felt messed with. I felt insane.

I was angry when I realized how brainwashed I had been. My blog writing naturally reflected that, exposing the Hell that Freedom Village was and how lost and ignorant we all were. Then other ex-Villagers began to reach out to me about their own experiences—good experiences. Many people who had worked as staff told me that they had disagreed with so much of Freedom Village's culture, but they stayed because they didn't want to leave troubled teenagers in a toxic atmosphere. I recalled how I saw staff members many times try to challenge or change the system, but they ultimately were fired. At the time, I'd been convinced these employees were Satanists who wanted to take us all down, so it was a blessing when our pastor got rid of them.

My parents remained supportive as I published these new blog posts, but they also pushed back on my perspective that Freedom Village was pure Hell. It opened my mind even further: Good things did happen at this place. Teens who needed help came to Freedom Village, and people came to work there to help them. Those helpers urged me to understand that they had wanted to be part of a solution. Others who had gone through the program at Freedom Village as teenagers admonished me for speaking badly of it. They said their lives had been saved there, forever changed. They claimed to have met God at Freedom Village.

I started to grasp that the brainwashing I experienced while growing up in Freedom Village was not universal in its intensity. I was, perhaps, one of the people most saturated with its toxic traits, merely because Freedom Village was quite literally the only atmosphere I had known since birth. Nearly everyone else had lived outside this community and without its leader for some part of their life, offering them a perspective that I was unable to achieve while there.

AS I GRAPPLED with what Freedom Village was, I kept writing my story, as honestly as I possibly could. This process was like a light, gradually exposing the darkness in my mind.

I learned about myself and my experience alongside my blog readers. My stories seemed to center around one man: the founder, visionary, and self-proclaimed pastor of Freedom Village. I began to see this man more clearly because I allowed for the possibility that he was *not*, in fact, a man of God. And by the end of those posts, a miracle happened: I saw this pastor as he was, and I lost my fear of him. This change is the driving force behind this memoir. I am not interested in revenge. I am not interested in fame. I certainly do not want pity. I do want to get even—but perhaps not in the way you would expect.

We typically think of getting even as the act of hurting someone as much as they have hurt us...then we're even. We want an eye for an eye, so to speak. Growing up, I read Bible verses about God lifting up the lowly and bringing down the prideful. In my mind, that always meant that I am righteous, so God will bring the wicked, prideful people down beneath me. I will be lifted up, and they will be punished. These days, I know God through the lens of Christ. In the reality of Christ, we are all the same. We all fall short, and we are all forgiven, not because of anything we can do or be but because of who God is. Nobody is over or under anyone else, and no one is better or worse than anyone else. I am certain that if my former pastor believed that, he would be saved, too.

Perhaps God lifts up the oppressed and brings down the oppressor not to create just another me-above-you dynamic but instead to allow us to see each other clearly, in equal standing. To *get even.*

As I accepted the tension between the good and evil of Freedom Village, I saw its leader exactly as he was…just a human being, the same as me. With that, my fear is gone. In its place is grief and grace, for all of us.

WEDGED within the sixty-six books that Christians call the Holy Bible is a tiny, three-chapter book called Habakkuk. Habakkuk was a Jewish prophet who lived around 600 BC. What I love about this guy is that he was a seeker, and he asked God some really hard questions. He lived in a time when it appeared God had abandoned His people. The wicked were thriving. Justice was nowhere to be found. The poor were oppressed. The weary were burdened. And Habakkuk wanted to know why God was letting it all happen and, perhaps more important, how long God was going to let it go on. Amazingly, God welcomed his inquisition; not once is Habakkuk rebuked for his questioning.

> **Habakkuk's Complaint**
> "How long, Lord, must I call for help, but you do
>   not listen? Or cry out to you, 'Violence!' but
>   you do not save?
> Why do you make me look at injustice?
> Why do you tolerate wrongdoing?
> Destruction and violence are before me; there is
>   strife, and conflict abounds. Therefore the law
>   is paralyzed, and justice never prevails. The

wicked hem in the righteous, so that justice is perverted."

The Lord's Answer

"Look at the nations and watch—and be utterly amazed. For I am going to do something in your days that you would not believe, even if you were told."

—*Habakkuk 1:2-5*

Habakkuk's prayer of "How long, Lord?" has often accompanied my thoughts about my former pastor since I left Freedom Village. How long will he avoid taking any responsibility for his actions? How long will he continue to cause harm? Ex-Villagers' allegations and lawsuits against this man span many types of abuse. No amount of truth-telling or exposure appears to have swayed him toward what I would call repentance or significant legal accountability. My anger at this led me to question: Do I want this man to see himself clearly so that he will be condemned and punished, or so that he will be set free from the hell he has created for himself?

I believe in mercy. I have no problem receiving the grace that God pours out each day. It's in that same spirit that I can freely give grace away. In my receipt of grace, I have begun to learn about the heart of God and His unconditional love for all of us. I have discovered a truth that has changed my mind, my perspective, and much of my worldview. The true God saves both the oppressed and the oppressor. I want to be like this God. Call it absurd, but I am going after the heart of God.

In this book, you will read stories of my own life. Here I tell the truth, like I always have. I expose secrets that have managed to stay hidden until now. My words reveal the darkness—*not* to bring shame or condemnation but to expel that very darkness, which has obscured the truth from so many for so long. I've found that the truth really does set us free, and the truth won't hurt what it won't also heal. I hope my words bring healing to both the oppressed and the oppressor.

THIS BOOK TELLS MY TRUTH: what it was like to be born and raised and to work in Freedom Village USA, and what it was like to leave and to rediscover faith on the outside. I have chosen to tell this story now because I can see the purpose deep within my suffering.

I believe my destiny was written and finished before I was born. I had no control over the year I would be born, the parents I would have, the country and culture I would be born into, the frame of my body, the color of my eyes. I believe that all of it was predetermined so that I might live out my purpose. My suffering at Freedom Village, and my redemption after I left, was my path to seek and find the heart of God.

I'm finally able to acknowledge and honor the truth that Freedom Village was where many traumatized people encountered God in a profound way and began to heal. It's also true that nearly all of what has traumatized *me* is directly linked to Freedom Village. How can two things, so seemingly contradictory, coexist? Where was God for those of us who suffered?

Like Habakkuk, I've been relentlessly seeking answers to the hard questions. God's response to Habakkuk is the foundation of this book: *Look, watch, and be amazed. What I'm doing in your life—well, you wouldn't believe me if I told you.* Like Habakkuk, I needed to see and experience the truth. The result was pure belief.

This book is for anyone who reads it, but I confess I have a special place in my heart for those of you who were at Freedom

Village. I've heard from enough of you to know that we all have an undefinable bond. I know that many of you feel insane. I know that many of you walked away from Freedom Village and are trying to never look back. I know that many of you wondered where God was during our time there. So did I.

I'm a born seeker, however, and the best part about seeking is finding. What I found is something I wouldn't have believed, even if you told me.

I cannot tell you what to believe about Freedom Village. It's not a simple place to understand. All I can do is tell you my story and let you decide what *you* believe.

Buckle up. It's a wild ride.

1

FREEDOM VILLAGE USA

NEITHER OF MY parents grew up particularly religious; they weren't people you'd expect to go into a life of full-time ministry. My dad was a divorced father of two. He was a touring musician who spent most of his time in nightclubs. My mom was an actress, singer, and dancer at Radio City Music Hall who had recently converted from Satanism to Christianity. She wasn't a Rockette, but my mom sang, acted, and danced with many Radio City productions. She met my father in Ohio while on tour with the musical *Godspell* in 1977.

Shortly after they became a couple, my dad became a Christian as well. My parents left the world of show business behind, relocated upstate, and got married. My dad worked as a salesman in a music store, where my mom taught piano lessons. They joined a tiny church and grew deeply in their faith. Eventually, they surrendered their lives together at the altar, committing to whatever God wanted them to do.

In 1981, before I was even born, a man came to my parents' church in search of staff members for a full-time Christian ministry for troubled teens. He was a massive man, both in physicality and personality. He stood well over six feet tall, with broad shoulders and prematurely graying hair. He oozed charisma, exuded power, and demanded respect simply by walking into a room. My parents were not the only ones drawn to this man's vision of helping lost teenagers.

His name was Pastor.

He had another name, of course, and you can easily find it if you want to. I've decided not to use his real name in this book. Within his ministry, we had little choice about we called him: It was simply "Pastor." I never heard anyone call this man by his name. He created an entire ministry full of adults and children alike who called him only by his title. It seemed perfectly normal to me growing up there, but out here in the real world, I've never come across that in church spaces. Most pastors include a name, like Pastor Tom or Pastor Brown. But not at Freedom Village. *Everyone* called him Pastor.

Pastor was a self-proclaimed—not ordained—preacher. Unbeknownst to his audience at my parents' church in upstate New York, he had recently left behind embittered followers at his church, Gates Community Chapel of Rochester, Inc. Journalist Michael Ziegler recalled speaking to members of Pastor's congregation in 1981, writing later in the (*New York*) *Democrat and Chronicle*: "I expected the members of his home church on Brooks Avenue to be highly devoted to [Pastor]. Instead, they were disillusioned and bitter, citing example after example of financial abuses and bum debts that raised serious questions about [Pastor's] honesty." Pastor left the Rochester church and registered a "doing business as" name under the tax-exempt organization of his Gates Community Chapel. He set his sights on Lakemont, New York, where he said God had given him a vision for opening a home for troubled teenagers: Freedom Village USA.

Pastor was certainly not the first or the last to start a program whose stated mission was to rescue America's troubled youth. Lester Roloff, a fundamentalist Christian, was widely influential in creating the troubled teen industry by opening homes for wayward teenagers in Texas in the late 1960s. Following allegations of abuse at these homes, documented in publications like the *New York Times*, Roloff famously refused on religious grounds to cooperate with state requirements to obtain an operating license and allow in welfare inspectors. Many troubled teen programs and Christian ministries that exist today still function in the same way. They claim to have "the answer" for troubled youth, an answer that often involves corporal punishment, isolation tactics, and consistent religious programming.

Pastor also refused to have Freedom Village licensed by the State of New York. It's one of the most sinister things about Christian troubled youth programs: There's a strange pride that some have in refusing to be licensed by the state because of their convictions. I was under the impression that if Freedom Village became licensed by the state, we would be giving control over to the God-haters within the government. The lack of a state license kept the government out of our program's business, and it also provided a way for minimal legal accountability for the practices of Freedom Village.

Freedom Village was closely patterned after Roloff's wayward teen homes. The focus was on teenagers whose backgrounds were a patchwork of bad circumstances, broken homes, and personal rebellion. The youths would commit to a year in the program, which was heavily steeped in the culture of church, Scripture, counseling, Christian schooling, and an array of other activities.

Located on an old college campus overlooking Seneca Lake in the rural Finger Lakes wine country, the property had two dormitories, two office buildings, a football field, a cafeteria, a chapel, and various on-campus staff homes. The campus had full-time security. The ministry also purchased several homes located close to campus, meaning that virtually anyone who worked at Freedom Village lived in a staff home owned by the ministry.

On the surface, Pastor offered Christians like my parents a way to devote their lives to helping teenagers. He marketed Freedom Village as a faith-based rehabilitation program and claimed that its "high success rate" was because the children and young adults were given a choice and had decided to commit to attending.

The catch was that once a teenager came to Freedom Village, they were all but denied the choice to leave. I lived at Freedom Village for two-thirds of its thirty-seven-year existence and saw thousands of teenagers and young adults go through the program. I can think of perhaps only thirty people who managed to leave on good terms and remain a friend of the ministry on the outside. Once you came to Freedom Village, whether as a troubled teenager or a staff member, you surrendered your free will under the guise of "honoring your spiritual authorities"—a concept supported by Scripture. In practical terms, if a teen in the program felt that leaving was the right thing to do but someone in a leadership position disagreed, the teen was biblically obligated to defer to the authority of the leader. If they left Freedom Village anyway, it was on bad terms, and everyone knew it.

Mixed into the mess, however, were many staff families like mine, who truly believed they were doing good things. Programs to help at-risk youth aren't necessarily staffed with sick-minded, abusive individuals, though it certainly offers an ideal environment for people like that to thrive. But there was also good there. God was there. I know this because Freedom Village had people, like my mom and dad, who joined the ministry to help people. The problem within the ministry was a lack of discernment—brainwashing—an inability to realize that Pastor's intentions were not godly. When something is godly, the root of it is love. At the root of Pastor's leadership was fear. When fear is in the mix, even something meant for good becomes tainted and twisted. It causes harm instead of healing.

Pastor set *many* rules and standards, and he expected them to be upheld by everyone: program teens, staff, the children of staff, and even visitors. Every rule at Freedom Village was supposedly based on the Bible; little did I know, my worldview was based merely on Pastor's *interpretations* of the Bible. Each one of his rules had a corresponding punishment if it was broken. The rules were very effective. Obedience to Pastor's ways, disguised as God's ways of holy living, resulted in a curated culture of people who all looked, acted, spoke, sang, and served in a way Pastor approved of.

AS YOU MIGHT IMAGINE, appearance was a crucial aspect of the rules and expectations at Freedom Village. Girls and women had to be feminine and pretty but not so attractive that we were distracting. We had to dress modestly; no form-fitting clothing was allowed. Shirts had to hang loosely off the chest so no curves could be seen. Shirt collars could not be lower than three finger-widths below the collarbone. If Pastor thought any female's clothes were too tight, he would tell her to change. Nine times out of ten, he received obedience without question. If his standards were questioned, there would be Hell to pay.

Until I was eight or nine years old, girls and women were not allowed to wear pants; we only wore skirts and dresses. Pastor's mindset on this came from Deuteronomy 22:5—"a woman must not wear men's clothing"—and he considered it a sin. That is, until his wife wanted to wear pants. And just like that, we *could* wear pants. They had to be loose, baggy enough that we could grab a handful at the top of each leg, yet they couldn't touch or drag on the ground. Imagine how cute those jeans were: saggy and bootcut.

In order to uphold the modesty standards, girls and women had even more rules to follow. We had to lift our arms up to ensure no stomach was showing. We could wear sleeveless shirts only if the shoulder straps were at least three fingers wide. If we were wearing a skirt or a dress, we had to kneel and make sure the fabric was *pooling* on the ground, not just touching it.

We were not allowed to have wet hair; Pastor said it made men lustful because it looked like we had just been in the shower. He also forbade all Black and Brown children and adults from wearing braids. This was horrific for new girls who, not knowing the rules, arrived on their intake day having just had their hair done in beautiful, elaborate braids. They had to take out their braids immediately because Pastor didn't like how they looked. Racism was undeniably woven through the rules of his program and the way he treated people in general. I personally witnessed Pastor's racist comments and actions many times.

As it usually goes in both religious and mainstream cultural systems, there were far fewer rules for boys' and men's appearances. They were expected to be clean-cut and masculine. Pastor expressed extreme disgust for homosexual people, particularly males. He seemed to hate nothing more than an "effeminate man," and that hatred informed many of the rules and structures at Freedom Village. Regardless of whether we personally agreed with Pastor's particular flavor of fundamentalist Baptist convictions, we all were expected to live by, uphold, and enforce his belief system. He believed interracial dating was a sin; therefore, no one at Freedom Village was allowed to date a person of another race. He believed homosexuality was a sin, so same-sex attraction was not tolerated; it was punished.

Pastor found a way to create a world filled with people who acted exactly the way he wanted them to. He didn't have to coexist with anyone who behaved in any way he disliked; he didn't have to experience accountability or true adversity in any way. I believe this unnatural way of life hurt him; it hurt the rest of us who gave him exactly what he asked for, too.

As a child who never knew any atmosphere but the one at Freedom Village, I believed this man wholeheartedly. I believed that his purpose in life was to teach me about God and develop me in my faith. I trusted Pastor's teachings as true, especially because I was raised in a concentrated community of people living in full obedience to him. Everyone wanted to serve God. I believed that in order to serve God, I needed to obey my pastor, because God had placed him in a position of spiritual leadership. I didn't question *any* of his teachings. I never wanted to rebel against the rules. In my mind, disobeying Pastor's rules was the same thing as breaking God's laws. Likewise, the rules for teenagers in the program were cloaked in Scripture. Were they Pastor's rules, or were they God's laws? If you obeyed the rules of Freedom Village, you were rewarded with privileges; if you obeyed God's biblical laws, you would earn His favor and blessings. It was all the same.

THE PROGRAM for troubled teens at Freedom Village was built on a system of levels named primarily for the acronym of the Christian school curriculum we used: ACE, or Accelerated Christian Education. As kids in the program progressed, they earned more levels of trust, which translated to more responsibility or work.

<u>Freedom Village Levels System</u>
Senior Staff
Junior Staff
Pastor's Club Monitor
Pastor's Club
E Level
C Level
A Level
No Level

When teens entered the program, they were placed on the neutral C Level. Their ascent or descent from that level depended solely on their behavior. If they obeyed the rules, they would be promoted to E Level. E Level came with rewards, such as a special treat or privilege. If they continued to follow the rules, they would be promoted to a level called Pastor's Club. Perks for Pastor's Club included time with Pastor, such as cookouts at his house, and leadership roles in their dormitory. The next level up was Pastor's Club Monitor, which meant you had all the benefits of Pastor's Club, plus you could monitor other program kids. This was the first level where kids began to have staff-like responsibilities—effectively, unqualified teenagers were being groomed as staff in the name of leadership potential. Once kids had been successful in the program for close to a year, they could become Junior Staff, taking on most of the responsibilities of a staff member without being on the payroll. If they had graduated high school and wanted to stay, they could be promoted to Senior Staff. Rising through the Levels System was not an objective process but rather based on favoritism, and it turned program kids against one another. Young people were overworked without any pay. The goals were to reward obedience and conformity and to punish disobedience and autonomy.

If a newcomer disobeyed the rules, they would drop from C Level to A Level. A Level meant facing restriction from certain activities. But the lowest and most dreaded level of all was No Level. If someone reached No Level, they had to haul wood.

This punishment was exactly what it sounds like: Teenagers carried logs in a circle. It didn't have any productive purpose; they weren't hauling logs from the trees to a wood-burning stove or anything like that. There was simply a circular path to walk again and again while carrying wood until their time was up. On both sides of the campus were big piles of small to medium-sized logs that were heavy and awkward to hold. The boys' wood pile was on the south side of the campus and the girls' on the north, both in plain view of everyone at Freedom Village. Kids who had reached No Level would have to walk in circles. They would carry a log for one loop, drop the log, walk around the circle again without the log, pick up the log, and repeat. This punishment was executed from five to six each morning and from six to eight each night. These kids also sat at their own No Level table in the cafeteria for all meals, where they were monitored and not permitted to speak.

Anyone, including staff kids and Junior Staff, could be written up if their behavior violated the Freedom Village code of conduct. Everyone living at Freedom Village was expected not to swear or curse. Program kids had to do chores without complaining. No one was allowed to talk about their past in a "glorifying" way. They had to read their Bible daily and prove they had done so by taking notes, which had to be turned in after every personal quiet time, chapel, or church service. There was absolutely no contact with the opposite sex. Program girls and boys were not even allowed to look at each other unless they had been granted such privileges by Pastor. Lying, cheating, gossiping, talking back to an authority, and even questioning authority were all punishable offenses.

Every person on staff was required to work a dorm shift, where they would personally oversee the program students. Junior and Senior Staff would enforce dress code checks and chores. Every student was required to write weekly letters, which were opened, read, and approved by staff before being sent home. Staff monitored every phone call from program students to their parents. If they said anything negative about Freedom Village, the staff member was required to end the phone call. Following these abrupt hang-ups, staff would cover up the comment, reminding the program student's family that the teen was, after all, troubled. If anyone is troubled *now*, it's me, knowing that I grew up to be complicit in these practices.

The rules were upheld at Freedom Village through fear of punishment. If any staff member, at any time, saw someone break a rule, they would fill out a write-up slip describing the offense. These write-ups would be read aloud every morning after chapel service in front of everyone. If you did something wrong, it would be loudly proclaimed in front of every staff kid, program teen, and staff member. Sometimes the program deans would read these, but those times were rare. Pastor himself wanted to read the write-up slips. He would then dole out punishments publicly. If you got into trouble, your level would drop. How far it dropped was up to Pastor. Someone on E Level could be written up for lying, and they could drop to A Level. Some offenses were more scandalous than others. I saw people fall from Junior Staff straight to No Level. Each punishment involved a drop in the Levels System, encouraging shame as a behavior modifier and furthering the atmosphere of favoritism and division. The lower your level, the fewer privileges you enjoyed. No Level was the worst of the worst. Being on No Level essentially meant having no life. The period of time for this punishment was also determined by Pastor. I saw people receive anywhere from one day to ten weeks of No Level.

ONCE A YOUNG PERSON climbed the Levels System, the possibility emerged for dating, as long as the relationship was approved by Pastor. If both parties reached Pastor's Club, a program boy could ask for Talking Permission with a program girl. When two people wanted to start "talking," the boy would have to go to the front of the church where we had morning chapel and church services, get on one knee, and ask Pastor for Talking Permission. If Pastor granted the request, that couple would be allowed thirty minutes per day to talk in the cafeteria at lunchtime. There was no other interaction allowed. Even with Talking Permission, every couple had to obey the Six-Inch Rule, meaning that partners couldn't come within six inches of each other. No kissing. No hugging. No holding hands. No sitting closer than six inches.

The next step of a relationship was Dating Permission. This was usually only attainable if the couple had both reached Junior Staff. Dating Permission was also requested by the boy, on his knee, in front of everyone. If granted, the couple could sit together in church services and chapel and even go on occasional dates. *Everything* was chaperoned though. Couples with Dating Permission were never allowed to be alone; everything was seen by everyone.

Pastor was the only one who could permit anyone to date, and he could also put a stop to any relationship at any time. If someone with Talking or Dating Permission got written up, Pastor would read their offense aloud and, many times, punish them by taking away their relationship with their significant other. He alone determined the amount of time until they could speak or date again.

MARY ROSENBERGER

AT FREEDOM VILLAGE, an active spiritual life was not suggested; it was enforced. It was clear that the only way to progress through the program was to adapt to the spiritual atmosphere. People who did not profess faith in Jesus simply didn't move up the Levels System and could not earn leadership and privileges. Scripture reading and memorization was required. Each month, every program teen and staff kid was required to memorize a specific passage of Scripture that was ten to fifteen verses long. Before chapel service each morning, we would all stand with our Bibles open and read the passage out loud. However, there was a large incentive to memorize it: Once you did, you got to sit down. Anyone with a good memory would recite the verse as soon as possible. By the time we were two-thirds through the month, only a few poor souls were left standing and reading Scripture out loud. This created an atmosphere of fear and shame, which was especially damaging for those already struggling with low self-worth.

In this environment, I was taught that there was only one way to Heaven, and it was the same way one could survive Freedom Village. One of my worst fears was being kicked out of Freedom Village, which was the penalty if someone consistently questioned the rules and systems of the ministry and of Pastor. To have any chance of happiness in my life, I needed to believe what I was told to believe. If someone claimed to believe in Jesus, but their doctrine didn't line up with Pastor's, I was convinced that they were deceived by the Devil.

My survival as a child and even a young adult depended on believing and confessing the "right" things. It's impossible for me to know how many spiritual lives were genuine at Freedom Village and how many were simply the survival skills of frightened people who presented such to earn favor from Pastor and the staff. I understand now that many people who went through the program faced more than spiritual abuse. I believe it. But I cannot tell those stories because they're not mine. The story I'm telling is about the abuse I endured from a man who claimed to love me.

As a little kid, I thought it was normal to be afraid of your religious leader. I didn't realize that I equated Pastor's approval with God's approval in my mind and my heart. For as long as I knew him, I was torn between wanting Pastor's attention and approval and simply wanting to disappear because I was afraid he would find something wrong with me. In my mind, Pastor's standards *were* God's standards. To question his spiritual authority was to question God Himself. To me, Pastor *was* God, and I lived in fear of him. Oddly enough, this all felt right and normal. I was supposed to want to please God, right? And if this man was appointed by God to be my spiritual authority, then I was pleasing God by obeying Pastor.

I was the perfect prey.

2

OBEDIENCE BRINGS BLESSINGS; DISOBEDIENCE BRINGS CONSEQUENCES

MY PARENTS JOINED Freedom Village as one of the first ministry families and moved to Lakemont with my two-year-old sister in 1982. My dad put his knack for sales to good use as a fundraiser for the ministry. My mom helped build the music department, which began as a choir for the program teens. This choir grew into the Victory Singers, a traveling singing group that would later tour all over the US and Canada to solicit donations. My brother was born a few years after they moved, in 1985, and by the time I came along in 1987, Freedom Village had really gained momentum.

Ours was one of ten or fifteen staff families at Freedom Village. Even though my family lived off-campus, in one of the nearby staff homes owned by the ministry, the community was designed to encompass us in a contained way. There was a school on the campus for the children of employees, taught by Freedom Village staff. My siblings, friends, and I were called staff kids. In my earliest years, Freedom Village was an easy place to be a kid. I went to school and church, played with my friends, explored the ministry's campus, and tagged along on singing tours with my mom.

Everything centered on Jesus. I grew up around many teenagers at the end of their ropes—people Jesus would have referred to as "poor in spirit." Many of the program teens likely assimilated into the religious culture in order to survive. But I also witnessed many real-time transformations of the heart and mind, and I credit that to God alone. I saw God move and work often in my life at Freedom Village, healing spiritual wounds.

From a very young age, I was well-informed about the program teenagers' "crazy pasts." Even though I wasn't integrated with the program teens much at that point, I can't count the number of times one of them told me, "You're so lucky you're a staff kid. Your life is so perfect! I wish my family were just like yours." And honestly, my life wasn't bad then. When I was little, I remember being happy. I had good friends and a huge, close-knit community of people looking out for me. Everyone knew everyone, and everyone was like family.

When I was seven or eight years old, I found out that a staff family was moving away, one of my friends with them. This is the first memory I have of a close friend leaving Freedom Village. It felt abrupt and as scandalous as my young mind could comprehend. This wasn't a childhood friendship that could survive long distances by writing letters after one kid moves away. Even that young, I believed her family was very wrong. Leaving Freedom Village was tantamount to disobeying God.

Even had I wanted to keep up a relationship, it was not an option. There was no exiting Freedom Village peacefully. All contact with families who had left the ministry was literally forbidden. Once they were gone, a smear campaign began. Rumors blazed around the entire ministry like wildfire. I heard that my friend's mom "wore the pants" in the marriage, and her husband couldn't stand up to her enough to keep them in God's will. I saw everyone through the lens of Pastor's so-called biblical standards, which included the importance of a stereotypical patriarchal family structure. Given the rumors about her family and my own sense of their mistaken decision, I didn't want to keep in touch with my friend anyway. From then on, every time another staff kid who was a close friend left with their family, it was as if they had died, and my next friendship was a little less deep. Never once did it even *begin* to occur to me that I was being manipulated into cutting ties with people I loved. It felt like somehow I was being virtuous by ending the relationship.

One time, another staff family left Freedom Village, taking more of my friends along with them. A few years later, their mom died of cancer. More than once, Pastor preached to us that she died because their family left God's will—meaning his ministry. The situation underscored one of Pastor's most repeated messages: "Obedience brings blessings; disobedience brings consequences." I took this to mean, "If you obey God, you will earn His blessings; if you disobey Him, *be very afraid.*"

I watched so many families come and go. After each left, we all heard stories of how their families were destroyed out there in the real world...out from under the umbrella of God's will. What I didn't learn until I was older was that nearly everyone who ever left did so because of disagreements with Pastor. They questioned his authority or they refused to adhere to one of his rules, and they would be fired.

Pastor would then preach at church on Sunday about that family and assure us of what would happen to them. "Obedience brings blessings; disobedience brings consequences." I believed that I couldn't make it in the world beyond Freedom Village. This worldview was reaffirmed every time staff families returned after leaving, asking to work in Pastor's ministry again. Maybe they had lost a job or couldn't make ends meet, and back they'd be, kissing Pastor's feet and validating his warnings about how terrible and godless the real world was.

I OFTEN JOKE that if you want to know the essence of Pastor, imagine having Donald Trump as your religious leader: not for his political views but his charisma, the confident demeanor, the air of power and authority. It was clear that other people perceived him as important. More times than I can count, I watched Pastor enter a room—anywhere, a church sanctuary, a banquet hall, even a pizzeria—and people were swept up into his aura. He looked like an extremely strong man, not necessarily because of muscularity but because of his temperament. That said, I've seen him grab teenagers by their shirts and lift them a foot off the ground.

When I was nine or ten, I told my dad that I would hate him if we ever left Freedom Village. I remember this as clear as day. Just as the fault for leaving lay with my friends' families rather than with Pastor, I was ready to place all the blame on my own parents. I believe that the ministry included a calculated effort to create a culture where I would resent my parents instead of Pastor himself if my dad or mom ever questioned him or didn't let him lead (and control) our family. In that atmosphere, staff families were slowly broken and ripped apart. Wives were taught to be resentful of their husbands for not being "the man of the home," husbands were taught to be resentful of their wives if they "were a little too strong," and staff kids like me lived with the growing fear that their parents would make a mistake and get the whole family fired.

Pastor was the man who gave my parents their jobs and our family this incredible ministry, and for that, I grew up literally singing his praises. From the time I was nine or ten until the year I left, we would sing the classic '80s Christian hit "Thank You" by Ray Boltz as a real-time tribute to Pastor. The lyrics share the singer's dream of going to Heaven and witnessing people line up to thank his friend for his good works on Earth. At best, the song is an attempt to express gratitude for others. At worst, it's a theological cringe-fest that paints a picture of a heavenly afterlife where everyone lavishes praise on *us*. I can see why Pastor loved it, though: It was a perfect representation of his theology. He regularly preached about how those who did the most good in their lives would earn mansions in Heaven, and those who didn't serve God—or didn't serve Him well enough—would be given grass shacks. He actually said that: grass shacks.

My sister and Pastor's son were the lead vocalists for the Victory Singers, who would perform conservative Christian hits such as "Thank You." It strikes me now that my fear of Pastor was nothing compared to the fear I saw Pastor's son show. I have seen Pastor publicly hit his son, pick him up and slam him down, scream at him, criticize his weight, and in other ways belittle and humiliate him more times than I can count. Yet there this boy stood, leading a whole room in praise to his father. Pastor's son sang verses about all those in Heaven who would be lining up to thank this person who had done the most good. Then we all rose and joined in the last chorus, singing to Pastor about how thankful we were for what he was doing "for the Lord." Sobbing, we slowly walked toward the altar in front of the pulpit where he was standing, basking in the praise.

I cried my eyes out every time we sang "Thank You," trying to imagine a life without the ministry at Freedom Village and hating it. I was so grateful to Pastor. It's disturbing for me to realize that these were the moments of truest worship in my life...I just wasn't worshipping God. I don't know whether some people in the room rolled their eyes during this spectacle or if anyone was disturbed as they watched us praise and adore this man. But me? I was *all in*. My worship of God was essentially abstract. My worship of Pastor was central to my life. In my mind, Pastor was the reason my family was "in the will of God." He was the reason so many lost teenagers were able to find hope. He was our shepherd, he was the visionary, he was our leader, and I loved him. So I would walk to the front of the chapel, tears streaming down my face, as I was overwhelmed with gratitude for this man. You might think I was just an impressionable child then, but this same scene played out over and over again during my years as I grew up at Freedom Village.

I believed everything Pastor told me: That he was responsible for tens of thousands of souls coming to Christ. That one day, the only thing that would matter is how many souls I had won for Jesus. That thanks to him, we were able to dedicate our whole lives to winning souls for Jesus. I truly hoped that one day I would have an impressive mansion in Heaven and lines of people waiting to tell me how important I had been to them in my earthly life.

I was feeding the sickness that Pastor was infected with: fear. I believe the root of narcissism is the fear of being irrelevant or unimportant. The sinister thing about sickness is that it spreads. Pastor's fear and need to be important became my own fear and need to be important. I didn't want to be part of a family that rebelled against God by leaving Freedom Village. I wanted my family to be one of the most spiritually relevant families on Earth. I wanted to be valuable to God. I had to do it right. The cost of getting this wrong was too high.

This concern still manifests itself in me well into my thirties. I have fought long, hard battles against the fear that I will do something wrong, maybe without even realizing it, and I will cost my whole family God's blessings. The fear has led me to feel scrutinized by people one hundred percent of the time I'm around them.

If someone is upset with me, I have had a very hard time dealing with it. I've struggled with believing people are upset with me when, in fact, they aren't and have no reason to be. My childhood molded who I am today, and the process of untangling lies from the truth is ongoing.

One thing I know for certain: Pastor should have never been given power, influence, or authority over anyone. He's certainly not the first or the last charismatic person to convince the masses they should hand over their spiritual authority. I believe the story of Freedom Village is an extreme cautionary tale of what happens when a person gives spiritual authority to *anyone*. I accept that there are God-inspired reasons to have offices of leadership within the organization of the church, but my life has taught me that no one should ever spiritually rule over anyone else. All spiritual authority belongs to Christ, not to human leaders. If someone desires to be the source of God for another person, that's a massive red flag.

The girl I was would have never dared to dream of the day when she would publicly oppose Pastor and his teachings. I know that little girl was only doing what she needed to do to survive, so I honor her convictions. But I couldn't distinguish between obeying rules so that I could survive and maybe even enjoy life at Freedom Village, and obeying God's laws so that I could survive the end of time and enjoy life in Heaven. The punishments of man revealed the punishments of God, and the favor of man revealed the favor of God...or so I thought. But I've survived long enough to see fear for what it is and for what it's done to all of us at Freedom Village, beginning with Pastor as its first victim. It is compassion that drives me forward into waters that, if I'm honest, still scare me. If you're reading this, it means I published this memoir...and that means God's love has cast out even more fear from my heart.

3

SALVATION AND CONVICTION

AT AGE NINE, I got my first pair of pointe shoes. Those are the ballet slippers with a flattened toe that allow you to dance on the very tips of your toes. I had studied classical ballet since I was four, and now I was in pre-pointe classes, where we held onto the ballet barre for everything and barely raised up fully onto our shoes while we learned the basics. My pointe teacher forbade us from putting our shoes on at home to try to dance because we were only beginning our training in these new skills. We could seriously injure ourselves. She was right, of course. But I had exceptionally strong ankles, so I would secretly put my pointe shoes on at home and rise up onto my tiptoes over and over again. One Tuesday in the spring of 1996, I wore my pointe shoes at home—not for the first time—and successfully turned across my entire living room up on pointe! It was a big deal for me, but it was also reckless and dangerous.

I went to class that night, and my teacher asked us all, "Have any of you been wearing your pointe shoes at home unsupervised?" Everyone in class vehemently answered "No!"—including me. Instantly, I felt awful. I had such a soft heart, and not only had I disobeyed my teacher, but now I had lied, too.

Later that evening, at home, I went through the motions of eating dinner with my family. As I helped clean up the dishes, Billy Graham was preaching on the small TV in the kitchen. Anyone who has seen a Billy Graham crusade knows that when he invited people to come forward for prayer, they came by the thousands. I had watched Graham on TV many times before, and my own church had offered countless altar calls in my young life too. This night, though, was different. I had disobeyed and I had lied. As I watched people pour from their seats to repent at the altar, I actually caught his message. It was different from the one I heard in my church. Pastor preached, "God hates sin, and you are a sinner. Confess Him as Lord so you can be forgiven and go to Heaven when you die."

Graham's words were more like: "God *loves* you. He knows that we can choose between right and wrong, and that because of our human nature we will make wrong decisions. But God loves us so much that He made a way we could find redemption and forgiveness anywhere, anytime: sending His only Son to die upon a cross. Through that act, Jesus bridged the gap between fallen people and a holy God. The work is finished. Come by the way of the cross."

It wasn't as if this was the first time I had heard these words. Even though they didn't get preached in our church, my parents had shared them many times before. But they struck me as real on this night. All of a sudden, I was sure that if I died right at that moment, I would go to Hell because of the lie I had told my pointe teacher in our ballet studio. I was nine years old, and I felt deeply that I *deserved* to burn in Hell, which, for the unindoctrinated, happens to those who have not been saved—a moment of conviction when you choose to ask Jesus into your heart.

Tears ran down my face as I put away the dishes, as my actions grieved the heart of a God who loved me so much. I asked my mom to pray with me so that I could ask Jesus into my heart. I wanted so badly to be forgiven for something because I knew it could get me into trouble. And I did truly want to love God. I wanted to please Him. I would do whatever it took. I had heard of salvation prayers my whole life, and now it was my chance to pray mine. For a brief time, I felt not only saved but *safe*. My decision, after all, would make me all the more safe at Freedom Village.

Even just a few years ago, if you would have asked me when I got saved, I would have told you that it happened on this night when I was nine years old. Salvation isn't just a *part* of the church and Christian culture; it is the *reason* for it. What began as a genuine conversion experience thousands of years ago—in which people were converted *inwardly* from darkness to light by coming to understand the heart of God—has become a task that can be checked off if someone says they believe Jesus is Lord and joins a church. Growing up at Freedom Village, I considered salvation a one-time declaration of faith, not a process of transformation. These days, salvation and sanctification—the process of becoming more like Christ—go hand in hand. There was no starting point to my salvation, because the very process of knowing Christ *is* what is saving me. But I look back at my decision to follow Christ at such an early age and find a singular, coercive reason for my young "conversion" and my adherence to Christian beliefs: Hell.

Everything I learned about Hell in my life was conveyed through a Western, Southern Baptist, evangelical interpretation of Scripture. I was taught from birth that Hell was a place in the afterlife reserved for people who rejected God in one way or another in this life. There would even be many people in Hell who *thought* they were saved but got something wrong, and they would be damned right alongside those who had knowingly rejected

God. All that I believed was supported by Scripture, which I memorized and obsessed over in the name of "hiding God's Word in my heart." I believed in the End-Times, the Tribulation, and in the Rapture (the ascension of believers into Heaven upon Jesus's Second Coming) as young as five years old. I watched apocalyptic religious movies like *A Thief in the Night* and every version of *Left Behind*, a wildly popular Christian thriller series about the Rapture and its aftermath. At age nine, I was ready and willing to be beheaded for my proclamations of belief in Christ. I would do *anything* if it meant I would avoid burning in a lake of fire for eternity, surrounded by demons and infinitely separated from God.

Being raised in a saturated evangelical community like this, I knew that a one-time experience of salvation was central. It was clear such an event was an expected part of life. I saw the praise and celebration received by people who prayed the prayer of salvation. I knew there would come a day where I would make the decision I had heard so many people describe in their testimonies—their stories about sinning and then finding God.

The anticipated milestones of my life were learning to ride a bike, going to my first day of school, losing my first tooth, having my first crush, and getting saved. In Freedom Village, we were taught that this could happen when I crossed into the "age of accountability." According to Pastor, sometime between the ages of nine and twelve, I would start to desire bad things, or I would know something was wrong and do it anyway. Once you reached the age of accountability, if you died before salvation—before accepting Jesus as your Savior—you would go to Hell. Getting saved was easy enough though: You said a prayer, confessed your sins, and asked Jesus to come live in your heart.

I have looked back on that child version of myself and always felt that I had a pure heart. But decades later, my perspective has shifted. My heart was pure in wanting to be good, yes. However, there was *so much fear* in that heart as well. It makes sense that I crossed to the age of accountability at the earliest possible age: Nine years old was the soonest I could be certain to avoid Hell. From that point on, I relied on that conversion event as my ticket to Heaven when I died.

Salvation is central to most Christian doctrines; it might be part of yours. My exploration into salvation tends to stir up those who see the world through a narrow, black-and-white lens. I have finally made peace with others believing that my beliefs are wrong, and it is okay if that includes you. I am confident now that on that night after pointe class, I was not saved from anything other than my interpretation of Hell and the fear of an even more difficult life at Freedom Village. I believe I had a deep subconscious understanding that "making a decision for Christ" was also going to save me from the Hell of being seen and treated as an unbeliever within my community. I wanted to belong—to God and to my community.

Taking all of this into consideration, I can see that my motives for having a relationship with God were both pure *and* poisoned by fear. This is why I never truly had peace. Despite my Baptist doctrinal beliefs of "once saved, always saved," the atmosphere of people-pleasing at Freedom Village tortured me into white-knuckling my supposed assurance of salvation. I couldn't fathom having God's approval if Pastor disapproved of me.

I hope my one-time salvation story can serve as a cautionary warning as we nurture children in the church. If our mission to convert children to Christianity is poisoned by fear, it harms one of the most vulnerable groups of humanity: children.

Today, I believe that nothing can separate me from the God who created me, which is something *He* achieved on my behalf. By extension, this belief saves me in the afterlife, too, because even death cannot sever my union with the love of God. It is not my ability to believe that spares me from separation from God; it is a faithful, kind, compassionate, and long-suffering God who has united us, whether I choose to believe it or not. Salvation stops being a one-time experience when you believe you are always with God. Heaven is present within, and I am saved from Hell on Earth every single day.

4

DESCENT

EVEN THOUGH MY school classroom was separate from the program for troubled youth at Freedom Village, I was fully aware of all the program's rules by the time I was nine years old. Around then, many of those rules began bleeding into the staff families' lives. Unmarried men and women on staff couldn't date each other without Pastor's approval. Adult staff members had to go through Talking Permission to get to Dating Permission, abide by the Six-Inch Rule, and always be chaperoned when together. (As far as I know, no one dared to say, "No thanks, I will decide what I do with my own life." No one seemed to believe it was inappropriate for Pastor to dictate to adults who they could date and when they could start a relationship.)

By the time I was ten, every single rule of the ministry program applied one hundred percent of the time to staff families, whether you were on the clock or in your own home. This was also when I noticed something curious: Although Pastor created all of these rules for everyone, he didn't need to follow them.

Given my age, it was no surprise that no one said anything

directly to me, but still I heard the rumors that Pastor's wife had left him. I was under the impression that she was not a good woman, was not a good Christian, and had left Pastor all alone, and there was "nothing he could do about it." They weren't divorced, but even separation was frowned upon in our community. I never heard anyone question Pastor about it.

All of a sudden, Pastor had a girlfriend. She was a staff member who had moved to the ministry with her husband to help troubled teens. As I heard it, their marriage failed and they separated. When Pastor began dating this woman, there were again no questions, and many staff members welcomed his new relationship. From my perspective, it was as if his wife had disappeared into thin air. At the same time, Pastor continued preaching that it was sinful for any couple to be alone together, because only bad things come from allowing yourself to be tempted.

One night, while Pastor was dating this staff member, my dad drove by Pastor's house and saw his new girlfriend's car in the driveway. My dad went inside and found the two of them alone in the house. He had the nerve to tell Pastor to his face that it wasn't right to hold everyone else to a standard that he himself was not living up to. My dad—a man I'm confident was Pastor's only true friend—confronted him with the intention of helping him see that he had created a double standard.

One thing we were all taught repeatedly in church was that it is a terrible sin to "raise your hand against a man of God." The phrase is connected to the biblical story of David, who was being pursued by the appointed king, Saul. David refused to physically harm Saul, even though he was trying to kill David, because Saul had been anointed by God. At Freedom Village, to confront Pastor about his behavior was to question God Himself.

That was when the worst happened: My dad got fired. His act of accountability was seen as a threat to the spiritual authority and leadership Pastor held. My dad was given a letter saying he had been "terminated." That word is one of the clearest memories I have of this whole episode. I wondered, did "terminated" mean Pastor would take everything we owned? I knew we would get kicked out of the only house I had ever lived in, because Freedom Village owned our home. I would never see my friends again.

And we would be out of God's will. When other staff families left, I heard over and over the stories of their struggles in the real world: divorce, cancer, death of children, and general ruin (stories I came to find out only in recent years were lies). What would keep us from this same fate?

I think my parents tried to keep us in the dark about the firing, but I recall my mom and dad being in a state of desperation. Their calling was being threatened. How could any man kick them out of a place where God told them to be? My parents didn't want to leave Freedom Village. They wanted to stay at the ministry out of love for God and their obedience to Him.

Only Pastor could fire someone. He was also the only person who could let us stay there, and it would be out of the kindness of his heart. In the end, my father begged him to keep us by essentially telling Pastor that we *couldn't* leave. My dad's words were "God called us here, and only He can tell us when to leave." Still, even though Pastor actually could make us leave, he allowed us to stay.

I DON'T KNOW how much the other staff knew about my father's temporary termination. A few staff families left the ministry due to preexisting disagreements with Pastor; they wouldn't continue to live under his authority, no matter how much they wanted to help the kids in the program. Meanwhile, a lot of drama was brewing among the staff as Pastor's double standards became more blatant. Pastor was still married but had a girlfriend, and he offered no clear communication about how the staff were expected to handle this or to explain it to the program kids when questions arose.

Though no other staff members or program kids were permitted to bend the restrictions around dating, his new relationship sparked a shift in some rules that trickled down to the rest of us. Pastor's girlfriend, who eventually became his next wife, wanted to wear pants. For her, Pastor changed the rules for us all, and suddenly we could wear pants. My sense of confusion was profound. Children are traditionally not known for seeing moral shades of gray, and my own convictions were formed from Pastor's convictions. Because he had previously preached that it was morally wrong for a woman to wear pants, I believed it was sinful. When it suited him to change his mind, we were taught the opposite. It's no wonder my head was spinning.

This was just one small example of how Pastor used religion to push an agenda at Freedom Village. I'm still unraveling spiritual truths I was taught that I now see were not biblical; rather, they were rules made by a very human man. As disorienting as these revelations can be, they are always good news to me. Each time I realize that a piece of my faith foundation was built by man, I can joyfully release it and seek the truth from the Source.

MY DAD'S termination and reinstatement at Freedom Village caused some major shifts in my life.

The situation showed me who the boss of our family was. It wasn't either of my parents; it was Pastor. It might have seemed like my dad, or even God, made the decision for us to stay at

Freedom Village, but in my mind, Pastor alone had the power to let us stay or make us go. This sowed seeds of bitterness that were probably beyond all our awareness, in that the established father figure of our home was stolen from us. Pastor usurped his authority. The termination of my dad showed me that no matter how noble my father's efforts were, Pastor could reward us or destroy us. Perhaps in my father's mind, God had proven to be the ultimate authority, but this situation cemented my belief that Pastor held all spiritual (and practical) authority over my family.

Such a scene played out repeatedly in many staff families. Wives resented their husbands for not standing up to Pastor, and kids resented their parents for letting someone else parent them. It seemed like a calculated approach to control families by removing authority from its established place among families and couples. Using the name of God was an extremely effective means of persuasion. Pastor's position of leadership as the self-proclaimed spiritual authority allowed him to teach his own personal ideology as biblical truth, and it was consumed as such. He took Bible verses out of context and wielded them as a weapon against anyone he felt was beneath him. To me, this is the meaning of "taking the Lord's name in vain." Pastor seemed to be afraid of being in equal standing with others, so his teachings justified a "Kingdom of God" with a levels system...much like his own kingdom: Sober people were closer to God than people who drank alcohol. Straight people were holier than openly gay people. Men were above women; wives, mothers, and children were under the authority of the man of the house. Pastor's spiritual authority put him above us all, allowing him to override the authority he had granted to men in their own marriages and families. So many staff families believed living this way honored God.

The whole episode of my dad's firing made me resent my father for speaking against a man of God. I could not see the hypocrisy: that my father, not Pastor, may have done the godly thing. It taught me to never question a man of God, lest I find myself removed from Pastor's (or did I mean God's?) good graces. Someone looking at it from the outside might assume that my animosity would be directed at Pastor and my sympathies lay with my dad. In the reality I inhabited then, it actually caused me to feel more connected to and dependent on Pastor, while becoming more disconnected from and resentful of my own father.

I believe this incident put a target on my family members' backs that would remain in place as I entered my teenage years and until the day we all finally left, more than a decade later. I believe Pastor was jealous of my family, that he wanted and couldn't have what we had: a whole, unbroken family. After my dad's failed attempt at accountability, that jealousy became hatred. He hated us, and I believe that he wanted *us* to hate us too. He wanted my mom to hate my dad. He wanted my brother to hate my parents, and me and my sister to hate our brother. At Freedom Village, if someone showed backbone to Pastor, there was Hell to pay. Our Hell was more than thirty years of a very close, toxic relationship with a man who seemed intent on dividing and conquering our family, while publicly praising us for representing a godly home. It was profoundly confusing and spiritually disorienting. Despite being one of the few "founding families" at Freedom Village and one of the most long-standing, my family members would become the object of some of the worst abuse at Freedom Village. As is often the case, Pastor's abuse didn't look like abuse to us. Abusive people can be extremely convincing, appearing like they care deeply for their victims. As I got older, the abuse from Pastor would cause damage that ran deep, splintering my family apart and severing our emotional connections to one another, all while increasing our dependence on *him*.

5

MY SO-CALLED PERFECT LIFE

MY MOM HAD OPENED her own ballet school before I was born, and Pastor "allowed" her to keep the school even though, without a doubt, my parents would have closed the studio if he had ordered them to. I believe Pastor didn't make my mom shut down the studio because he was in love with controlling her, and we thus felt indebted to Pastor for the financial help the studio afforded us. I'd been dancing since I was four, and my mom was the one who most often trained me, but I didn't really take it seriously when I was young. Classical ballet drew me in when I became a teenager.

My motivation to become a better dancer flared the year our studio was doing a production of *Cinderella*. I desperately wanted the role of the Fairy Godmother. I thought I would get the part easily, despite being the worst-behaved kid in my mom's ballet class. I arrived at lessons late with my hair down and huge rips in my tights. I never paid attention, and even now, I can't be completely serious in a ballet class. I was always making everyone else laugh. It seemed my mom had had enough of me.

The day that casting decisions appeared on a sheet of paper taped to the wall in our studio, I rushed to see if she had given me the role I coveted. Instead, my best friend's name was listed beside the Fairy Godmother. She had started ballet much later than me but had a passion for it and a work ethic that put mine to shame. I frantically searched the cast list for my own name. Mary Siegfried: Winter Season Fairy. What a total letdown. I ran across the studio and threw myself into a chair in the waiting room to cry my eyes out. In hindsight, I can credit my mom for not just handing me everything I wanted without having to work for it. My friend completely deserved the part. Then and there I decided that I was going to take ballet seriously, and I did.

I started to live and breathe ballet: taking extra classes, stretching at home every day, and spending my summers going to ballet intensives. Intensives were like mini college experiences, filled with rigorous daylong classes where I was surrounded by kids just like me who wanted to improve their dancing. My first big intensive was in Jackson, Mississippi, at Ballet Magnificat, the world's largest professional Christian ballet company. Dancers from all over the globe attend their summer intensives. I flew there by myself when I was thirteen and stayed in a dormitory on campus for a four-week program. It was incredible, and I loved every minute of it.

Ballet Magnificat was the first thing I ever did outside of my bubble at Freedom Village. To this day, I can't believe Pastor gave the blessing for me to go. I'm not sure why he allowed it, but I am so glad for the whole experience. I went shopping for clothes, buying all kinds of outfits I thought were super cool. Little did I know that most kids in the real world could wear tight, strappy, and revealing clothes if they wanted. Even though I was going to a faraway city alone, where no one had even heard of Freedom Village, I had to follow the ministry's rules for appearance. I arrived in Mississippi, in long shorts that hit an inch above my knee and my overly conservative shirts, only to see the other teenage girls wearing cute short shorts and camisole tops. I felt weird and out of place, even at the same time I was judging everyone else for being immodest. There was such dissonance.

Looking back now, I wonder how I was even allowed to dance. It was a strange double standard that I had to wear abnormally modest clothes in public but could dance all day in a studio wearing nothing but a leotard and tights. There was definitely no dancing allowed in my church. More than a few times, Pastor preached passive-aggressively from the pulpit about what a waste it was to do anything just for pleasure. If it wasn't evangelical, it wasn't worth doing. And because we were being immodest while we danced, we couldn't win souls with it. Pastor never overtly mentioned my mom's ballet studio or even ballet at all, but I knew his stance. Everyone always knew exactly who he was talking about when Pastor preached a message about people.

Perhaps my mom redeemed her role as a dance instructor in his eyes with her work in music, since that was much easier to keep from being secular. She had founded and developed the Freedom Village music program, which began as a choir. Years later, she formed a small touring group of eight to twelve vocalists called the Victory Singers who would tour up and down the East Coast. They traveled across the US and Canada to both Christian and public schools, nursing homes, detention centers, jails and prisons, churches, festivals, town parades—you name it. The Victory Singers were teens who had progressed to E Level or higher, had made the salvation decision, and were considered spiritually "strong." Along with vocal performances, the group was trained to speak publicly so they could share their testimonies on tour. It was powerful to hear teenagers talk about the dramatic turnarounds they had made in their lives, always giving credit to God. But they were also giving the credit to someone else: Pastor.

In these kids' minds, the purpose of touring was purely evangelical. The singers wanted to save souls. But in reality, the goal of Victory Singers tours was financial. They took offerings, sold CDs and Pastor's books, and plugged Freedom Village's need for support. The singers' testimonies were used to bring funds into the ministry's bank account, all while they believed themselves elite Christian soldiers on the front lines of battle for the Lord.

As early as age three, I heard from those who saw my mom's singers perform that my family was so blessed. Others said how amazing my life must be or how they aspired to have my life one day. I remember feeling like a living trophy. And I can understand how my life looked perfect from the outside, particularly to the program youth, many of whom had been neglected or abused. My parents loved each other and had mutually decided to spend their lives in service to God. It certainly made me grateful for what I had, but it also created pressure to curate an ideal image of myself and my family. I was confusing my fear of imperfection with love for God.

Much of my family's image centered on music. Our Siegfried clan was known for being an incredibly musical family. My dad was a gifted musician, and my mom had a smooth, soothing low alto voice. My parents regularly sang in church together, my dad playing the guitar. They even produced and released a few cassette tapes of their music in the '90s. Many nights as I was growing up, my dad would put our cassette player at the bottom of our stairs with one of their tapes in it, and my siblings and I would fall asleep to the sound of our mom singing.

Nearly everything our family did revolved around music. My older sister, Sarah, is an incredible singer. She has one of the loudest, most powerful voices I have ever heard. I grew up watching her as the front woman for the Victory Singers. She then trained at the University of Rochester's Eastman School of Music with a prestigious voice teacher. As a pre-teen, I could hear Sarah practicing scales in her room and belting out strange vocal warm-ups in the evenings. Our brother, Jesse, is also musically inclined. He began singing and playing the guitar as a teenager and had a natural talent for both.

Coming of age in this very musical family, I had a lot to live up to. I sang my first solo in church when I was twelve, and I nearly threw up from nerves. It seemed like everyone expected so much from me musically because I was a Siegfried. I didn't have the confidence of my older siblings. And I had what was dubbed a sweet voice—not as strong and bold as my older sister's, but I could hold my own.

By the time I was thirteen, the Freedom Village music department was growing again. There were already two full-time touring groups: In addition to the Victory Singers, led by my mom, Sounds of Freedom was directed by a staff woman who had risen through the program. Now my sister Sarah was being promoted, from lead vocalist of the Victory Singers to director of another travel group for the touring music ministry, the New Life Singers.

Not only did I make it into this group when I was thirteen, but I found myself as the lead singer, news that was both exciting and extremely terrifying. I loved to sing, but I did *not* love to sing in front of people. Performing only created fear in me, although I soaked up the positive affirmation I received as a result of my singing. For a teenager who was uncomfortable being looked at, I often had to deny that feeling "for the greater good" when I sang. Love and fear were battling it out in a way that made true worship, as I know it now, very difficult.

Our New Life ensemble was made up of twelve teenagers, six boys and six girls, divided into sopranos, altos, tenors, and basses.

Despite being the youngest in the group, I carried a lot of musical responsibility, perhaps because I was also the only staff kid. I could at least be counted on not to leave Freedom Village anytime soon. When we performed, I led nearly every song vocally as the main soloist and had the responsibility of introducing our group in churches and schools. It was a lot of pressure, and, not coincidentally, I was quickly becoming a devoted people pleaser.

Still, I can honestly say that the early years touring with New Life were some of the best of my life. I had no idea then what an incredible opportunity it was to see the country. Every couple of weeks, I piled into a twelve-passenger van with all my best friends and toured for five or six days, singing at least one show before we stopped for the evening. Sometimes we would travel for a whole day, maybe to North Carolina, and the entire trip was spent laughing, fooling around, loading up on snacks at gas stations, and finally falling into our hotel beds late at night. The next morning, we would haul our equipment to a school, set up, perform our show, tear everything down, load up, travel to a detention center in the afternoon, and do it all over again. The New Life Singers got to stay in hotels, eat out at restaurants, and perform for hundreds of people a day, a much different experience than most of the teenagers at Freedom Village had.

Our musical group became close-knit, the way any kids spending that much time packed into a van do. But the individual faces of the group were always different, and again, many of my close friends disappeared from my life as they left Freedom Village. I even had occasional crushes on boys in New Life and was brokenhearted when they left the program, usually on bad terms. I wasn't allowed—nor did I want—to keep in contact with any of my friends who left our community. I found myself the one constant in the group, the stable core of an endless sea of changing faces.

The New Life Singers were essentially a touring poster for Freedom Village. The venues we performed in advertised our performances along the lines of "Come and see teenagers who have overcome their pasts and found radical transformation through the power of Jesus! Former drug addicts, prostitutes, and abused children all share their stories." And then there was random Mary Siegfried, plopped in the middle with her very ordinary (or so I thought) church-kid life.

Every show we did was a little different, and my sister gave us our set list about an hour before each performance. This is when we found out which songs we were singing for that show and who would be sharing their testimony. Our programs usually looked like this: opening song, welcome and introduction, three or four alternating songs and testimonies, an invitation to come forward for prayer and salvation, another song, taking up an offering, another song, and a closing song.

If I was on the schedule to share my testimony, horrible nerves would nearly get the better of me. I struggled the entire show, sweating, my hands shaking. When my turn came to speak, I wanted to crawl under a rock. But with the spotlight focused on me, I often shared a poem I'd written called "Through the Valley." The verses were about the twists and turns of life and how Jesus is always there, no matter what. I read that poem, usually through tears, despite the fact that I didn't know much about the true twists and turns of real life yet. But I always got through it. I reminded myself that it was not all about me but rather me sharing what God had done for me so far in life. My own testimony went something like this: "Even though I've been blessed to grow up in a Christian home with loving parents who are raising me right, I'm no better than anyone else. If I had died before I accepted Jesus as my Savior when I was nine, I would have gone to Hell, just like any drug addict or prostitute. I'm so grateful I am saved." With my plain salvation story, I was embarrassed that I didn't have a dramatic come-to-Jesus moment.

WITH THE NEW LIFE SINGERS, I sang through my stage fright and continued to share my personal testimony, despite my intense fear of public speaking. Ballet was another part of my life where I faced the conundrum of passion versus performance. I loved to dance, I loved classes, I loved rehearsals, I loved it all—until it came time to perform. I wanted to enjoy performing, but each time, fear and nerves overshadowed my passion. I'd leave performances frustrated and let down every time. What's more, no one knew this. I instinctively hid anything that could be perceived as a problem, which meant those around me were oblivious to my inner struggles. I'm sure everyone in my life believed I was confident and that I loved to perform. But these years of public performance sparked a new emotion that grew to become part of the fabric of me: anxiety.

Over the next couple of years, so many factors combined to take a toll on me. I was committed to dancing, singing, and sharing my testimony in performances that gave me intense anxiety. I heard time and again that I had the perfect life, adding more pressure to keep up the church-kid persona. But I didn't have the perfect life...no one does. Instead of acknowledging this truth, I filed away all of my shortcomings as "sins" and kept them hidden from the world. I silently suffered in shame each day from the moment I woke up to the moment I went to sleep. Of course, I didn't acknowledge those deep-seated feelings as unhealthy. I dismissed the weight of shame and anxiety as the cost of serving Jesus. It didn't matter how I felt; it only mattered that I pleased Him with my life.

6

DARKNESS

ONE DAY, my sister and I were walking out of an office building on campus as Pastor was walking in. He looked at me and, as usual, I shrank into myself. We all did that. One look from him and I would hunch my shoulders because I was afraid my shirt would look too tight. I thought if I avoided eye contact with him, he would leave me alone. By this point, around age fifteen, I had given up on always trying to make him like me; I just wanted him to forget I existed. No such luck that day.

"Mary, you look like you have some makeup on, there," Pastor said.

Before I could say anything, Sarah came to my rescue, grabbing my head and wiping her fingers—hard—across my eyelids.

"Nope!" she said. "No makeup here!"

I awkwardly laughed, and we left as quickly as possible.

We had recently gotten the news that Pastor had made a new rule: Staff kids couldn't wear any makeup until they turned sixteen. By this time, I had been wearing makeup, particularly my signature eyeliner, for years. I was completely mortified that I had to change my style to follow this new guideline, but we all did as we were told—mostly. I would put on mascara before bed, then not wash my face when I woke up so I could honestly say I hadn't put any makeup on that day. (This was the height of my teenage rebellion.)

The new makeup rule was just one example of Pastor's reach extending even further into staff families than before. He started to control staff members' kids and teenagers through the program rules, the same rules enforced for the program kids. I didn't know it at the time, but the year I was fifteen was the last year I'd attend a separate school on campus only for staff kids.

Everyone, especially teenagers, goes through hard things, but I was not prepared for any of what was coming my way. All throughout high school, I kept touring and performing with New Life. I took as many ballet classes as I could, going back to Ballet Magnificat every summer until I was eighteen. All the while, life was getting harder and more confusing at Freedom Village.

Around the time that I began touring, before he nearly caught me wearing makeup, Pastor started making staff kids haul wood. The punishment—hauling logs in a circle on campus for hours at a time—had previously been reserved for program kids. It was a humiliating punishment for staff kids, just as it surely was for the program teens, though it may have been even more confusing for us because it was handed to us by Pastor, not our parents. Their hands were tied. Many parents did push back, however, refusing to allow Pastor to dictate such consequences for their kids. Those families were fired or chose to leave on their own.

I hold firmly to the belief that the staff kids shouldn't have been subject to the program's regulations, because we weren't *in* the program. None of us chose to be at Freedom Village. We were kids, living under the supervision of our own families, not troubled teens who had willingly entered a program for support and direction. The rules within anyone's own home should never be controlled by religious leaders. It's unhealthy for the family and their internal relationships, and it's unhealthy for any leader to have that level of power. And that power differential had consequences beyond just the staff kids.

While there were many good people who worked at Freedom Village, there were also people with nothing better to do than make up lies and gossip about other staff, which kept them on Pastor's good side. Rumors spread about everyone all the time. If I confided in anyone other than my parents, I could count on that information to ultimately make its way to Pastor. From this rumor mill sprang my first blatantly disordered behavior.

When I was fourteen, a program boy I had a crush on left the ministry. Apparently, he spread rumors around the boys' dormitory that we had kissed, which wasn't true. Soon enough, that rumor made its way back to me. I was so terrified of what would happen to me, so aware of how humiliating that punishment would be, that I wanted to end my life. I cried and cried in my bedroom, thinking of any and all possible ways to kill myself. This wasn't for fear of repercussions by my parents but of how I would be dealt with by Pastor and Freedom Village. I was afraid he would put me in the program—a fear shared by many of the staff kids. Such an outcome would have meant ultimate control for Pastor for as long as my family lived at Freedom Village.

I was convinced that if I told anyone about my suicidal thoughts, I would shatter my perfect image. I would surely be taken out of the New Life Singers or even put into the program. These weren't irrational, far-fetched fears. It happened to my friends. I had watched program kids drop from Junior Staff down to No Level because of their "struggles with sin." And suicidal thoughts were definitely a sin. I couldn't let that happen to me.

As the rules that shaped the staff kids' world began to look more like the program kids', we grew ever more fearful of Pastor's authority and attention. It led me to develop a deep, paralyzing dread of people being upset with me. When I did get in trouble, I could hardly breathe. I wanted so badly to make everyone around me happy, but there was no pleasing this man, a man who controlled my entire life. Pastor could be your biggest fan one day and send you out to the woodpile to haul wood the next.

Things continued to go downhill for me as my school environment changed. When staff kids began going to school with the program kids—another new and arbitrary decree from Pastor—it seemed like just one more way for our lives to be dictated and controlled by the ministry. The first day my staff kid friends and I entered the program kids' schoolroom, it felt like the program kids were glad to see me in their world. Not because they liked me. I knew many of the program girls perceived me as stuck-up—not unfairly—and wanted to see me fail. I was friends with some of the program kids because I toured and sang with them. But for someone to be in a singing group, they would have been in the program long enough to rise through the Levels System and acclimate to Freedom Village's culture. They were at least Pastor's Club level, and most were Junior Staff. I hadn't spent a lot of time with the new or lower-level program kids until I walked into class that first day of my junior year of high school. I was a fish out of water.

Up until I was twelve years old, program kids told me, "I wish I were you." It happened so many times that I believed my life was perfect. Once I became a teenager and a peer to the program kids, "You have a perfect life" turned into "You think you're better than us." And, much as it pains me to admit it, they were right. Wasn't I better than them, somehow? My life was better than theirs had been. My parents were married and theirs were divorced or never married. My family served God full-time and their parents might not even be Christians. I believed *my life* was better. And on a spiritual level, I believed *I* was better: I was saved; they were unsaved. They were lost; I was found. My whole life was centered on saving lost souls...those lost souls just happened to be my peers now.

My relationship to the program kids was exposed for what it was once I entered my teen years. I viewed them the way a missionary kid might view another country's citizens who their parents want to convert. To me, the program kids needed to be saved. That salvation didn't really have anything to do with the here and now. I cared that they would go to Heaven when they died, not as much about what their physical or mental health looked like. I cared about helping them secure their eternal salvation, not as much about whether they felt loved or cared for here on Earth. All those earthly matters were secondary to the goal of "say this prayer and become a Christian." Then I could report to Pastor that I had won a soul to earn his favor. It's no wonder my connection to the program kids was mechanical and inauthentic.

This first year of my new educational environment I encountered a waking nightmare: I was accused of cheating in school. My principal went directly to Pastor without approaching me or my parents first. This type of backstabbing was literally rewarded at Freedom Village. I was punished before anyone even asked me about the false accusation.

After meeting with Pastor, the principal came to my classroom and told me publicly that I had been sentenced to two weeks of No Level for cheating. I was stunned. This meant I would have to haul wood with the No Level program girls from five to six a.m. and from six to eight p.m. every day for two weeks. It was obvious to me that my principal was getting some sick pleasure out of delivering the news to me. The whole ministry was going to enjoy seeing my fall from grace.

My image had been so carefully crafted: I was a good girl. This would never hold up in the face of such a public punishment—in front of my friends, all of the staff, and every single program kid. My parents had no say in the matter. The only way out of hauling wood would have been to leave Freedom Village, and that didn't seem to be an option. Whether that was because of the call of God or the power of brainwashing, I'm not sure I'll ever know.

The first night I was assigned to haul wood, I sobbed to my mom after dinner. I couldn't do it. The program girls who were also on No Level would laugh at me. I would be monitored by someone who was in the program. My mom cried with me and said she would walk the woodpile circle alongside me. I couldn't let her do that, as much as I wanted her to. I already knew that many of the program girls resented me for having a stable home life with loving parents. I wasn't about to let my mom walk the woodpile with me while the other girls either had no mom or one who might be hundreds of miles away.

I hauled wood every day for two weeks while drowning in embarrassment, shame, and confusion. I had no choice; my parents had no choice. As I walked around the woodpile, I prayed, trying to find meaning or purpose from God in the whole situation. The accusation of cheating and the resulting discipline threatened to tarnish my "good Christian girl" image, but I kept it up the only way I knew how: I obeyed Pastor and served my punishment, believing that it was all somehow for my good. I got through the woodpile, but I secretly became very, very depressed.

I WAS A TEENAGER—PERHAPS not a regular one, but a teenager nonetheless. I wanted to have as much fun as I was allowed to have. One night, my brother and I were invited to a friend's house with three other girls and another boy. We found ourselves playing a game of truth or dare, sitting in a circle on a trampoline in our friends' front yard. It was one of the rare moments in my life when I might have resembled an actual teenager. Our game was completely innocent—at least until one of my girlfriends brought up a sexual joke. I actually had no idea what it meant. The moment was quick, awkward, and unremarkable. The next day, one of my friends told a program girl about our game, and that girl went straight to Pastor's office to tell him. She said she intervened because she was "worried" for us and didn't want us to end up "like her."

Pastor immediately called all of us and our parents into a meeting to dole out our punishments. Two of my friends received ten weeks of No Level, whereas my brother and his friend were given five weeks of No Level and had their driver's licenses taken away. Somehow I got off "easy," with just two weeks of No Level. Again, despite the fact that our game had been played off-campus, our parents had no say over the penalties. Again, I hauled wood for two weeks. This time was easier because two of my best friends were serving their sentences along with me, but I was angry. I was angry at myself for doing something so wrong and so stupid.

I hated myself. I hated everyone else too. But not Pastor. Never Pastor. Perhaps logically I knew that Pastor was ultimately at fault for what I was going through. But my teenage brain turned all my blame inward. Well, maybe not all the blame. The program girl who tattled on us was certainly to blame. But she was human, fallen, prone to sin. And so was I. Was Pastor? At that point, I wasn't sure. Pastor had held himself out to be above the law—his own and God's—so many times that the lines were blurry. All I know was that I hated myself and I didn't hate him. I still wanted to please everyone. I wanted to be perfect. I needed to be the best to avoid feeling less than. Less than what? Pastor? Everyone else?

My own potential as a child of God? I believed I couldn't talk to anyone about my problems because I felt like I had no reason to be feeling this way. I was ashamed about having shame, regularly going into massive shame spirals.

Like most shame, mine couldn't be packaged up and compartmentalized. My shame carried into ballet, one of the things in my life that I still loved. I was in ballet class at the age of sixteen the first time I saw my body in a dysmorphic way.

"I look thick," I thought as I caught my reflection in the mirror.

In the world of classical ballet, everything revolves around long, lean lines. I wanted to look as thin as possible. God forbid a dancer's body thickens with growing muscle. The last thing a ballerina wants to look like is a gymnast. I determined that I would lose a few pounds. I decided to skip breakfast the day after my first intrusive thought in ballet class. The control felt wonderful. No one would know. No one *could* know.

I loved having a secret. At the same time, I was terrified because I had a secret. The shame I felt for dabbling with what I knew even then was an eating disorder propelled me to put even more of a perfect face on with everyone around me. I restricted my calorie intake until I was going days between meals. All the while, I kept singing and dancing for Jesus, I kept touring and praying with other kids on the road, I kept sharing my testimony, I kept winning Bible memory contests, and I kept getting perfect grades in school.

I was so proud—and so ashamed. My mind was breaking under the hypocrisy of it all. As it goes with many addictions, it happened slowly and then all at once. It's almost impossible to "dabble" with an eating disorder. It has hooks, and they go deep. Before I knew it, my mind was consumed with a nonstop thought process surrounding food and my body.

No one knew any of this, of course. I hid it well, but it didn't take long before people started to notice I was getting too thin. As soon as I realized that eyes were on me and my body weight, I went into performance mode, repeating a refrain of "I'm fine!" I evened out my eating habits to keep my problems hidden and to stay in control.

Not surprisingly, my attempts to be "fine" weren't working, and I had become even more depressed. My mom took me to the doctor because she noticed I had very little energy or motivation. He diagnosed me with clinical depression and tried to talk to us about prescription medication. Both my mom and I were stunned and offended. According to our beliefs, and Pastor's teachings, a Christian should never take medication for depression.

I had a hard time even accepting the reality of the diagnosis, because to me, depression was a sin. Hopelessness was the inevitable result of walking away from Jesus. Despair was the end of the road for someone who doesn't have faith. If depression was what happens to those without faith, how in the world could I be depressed? My entire life *was* my faith! Had I fallen through some spiritual crack? *What was wrong with me?*

For many Christians, the prize waiting at the end of this life is hearing "Well done, my good and faithful servant" from Jesus Himself. I'm not sure why the words Jesus spoke in the metaphorical parables recorded in the Gospel of Matthew became as literal for me as the resurrection, but it was an indisputable fact that Jesus Christ was waiting at the pearly gates of Heaven for each person as they arrived hoping to get in. At their appearance, Jesus would say one of two things: "Well done, my good and faithful servant" or "Depart from me, I never knew you!"

That alone was a terrifying thing to have hammered into my young psyche, but Pastor always made sure we knew the deep horrors of this wildly literal interpretation of Scripture. Not only would Jesus turn people away from Heaven in exclusion, but most of those rejected people would be people who *thought* they loved Jesus. Pastor would then go in for the spiritual kill, backing his claims up with his interpretation of Matthew 7:21: "Not everyone who says to me, 'Lord, Lord,' will enter the kingdom of Heaven." As a child, I was taught that those verses meant one thing: I could never actually know whether I was going to make it into Heaven. Even as I sang "blessed assurance, Jesus is mine" in church on Sundays, I never felt sure. I could think I was doing it all right, I could think I loved Jesus, and at the end of my life, to my great astonishment and horror, Jesus could cast me away, separate me from His love, and scream, "I never knew you, get away from me!" And here I was, depressed, a clear sign I was not pleasing God.

I turned to my journal to try to sort out the cognitive dissonance. Writing always exposes what is deep within me. I'd kept journals growing up, writing poems and documenting my childlike faith. By the time I received my offensive diagnosis of clinical depression, my journal already revealed the depth of my growing spiritual fear. I wasn't about to share any of *this* poetry. My writing had turned dark as I tunneled into my chaotic mind and attempted to process my secrets and my shame. I started writing *everything* in my journal. During these dark years, I sat in my room and wrote for hours, cataloging all the things I hated about myself.

The more I allowed myself to be honest there, the more I felt like a fraud everywhere else. I was the lead singer of a Christian singing group, touring and sharing my testimony, praying with kids all over the place to save their souls...and mine was a mess. *I* was a mess. That journal was filled with so much sadness, anger, confusion, and disorder. Several pages were covered in the words "I hate myself" over and over again. Where before I had written poems about Jesus and His unfailing love, I now wrote poems about ending my life, about what a disappointment I was to everyone, and about what a hypocrite I had become.

"Who does God hate?" someone might have asked me back then.

"Hypocrites," I would have replied. Yet there I was with my journal of secrets, the biggest hypocrite of all.

My spiritual life grew weak because shame convinced me that this sin was separating me from God. The voice in my head, which by no coincidence sounded exactly like Pastor's, told me that every time I sin, I hurt God. Believing that I was a walking offense to a holy God, I avoided prayer. I needed to have it all together before I approached God with either praise or petitions, and I was quickly realizing that I did not have it all together. Not at all.

Everything in my life was falling apart. I was plagued with anxiety, shame, and depression. Any benefit brought about by my singing was ruined because I felt like a hypocrite out on the road. My dancing suffered because I never ate enough food to have energy. My body image was horrible as I developed a severe case of body dysmorphia. My identity was crumbling because I had placed my value in what I *did* for Jesus, and I felt as if I were failing at all those things.

Around this time, I began to hear my parents fight, and I realized that their marriage was also under duress. Freedom Village was intended as a place for parents to hand to Pastor and his staff authority and control over their troubled teenagers. But he had extended his reach from the very beginning into staff families, and his decisions in recent years significantly usurped staff parents' authority and control over their own kids, placing Pastor between staff kids and their parents. Staff kids either hated their parents for not standing up to Pastor on their behalf, or, if they were like me, they hated their parents if they *did* stand up to him, because that opened up the possibility of being fired. He also seemed to systematically become a wedge that divided husbands from their wives. Families were falling apart, and even mine was not immune.

It was an open secret that Pastor had eyes for my mother. She certainly seemed to be his type: pretty, petite, talented, and another man's wife. I watched as Pastor seemed to delight in the struggles of my parents' marriage. By then I was the only kid left at home. My sister, Sarah, was living in her own apartment with another woman who worked at Freedom Village. She had graduated from high school and was staying on staff in the ministry, as nearly every other grown staff kid did. My brother, Jesse, had moved as far away from all of us as he could. Unlike me, he resented Freedom Village as a teenager. I believe Pastor treated my brother worse than any other staff kid, but that's his story to tell. My home life in those days consisted of me, alone in my room, as an ever-increasing foreboding spirit saturated our house.

One day, I was summoned from school to Pastor's office, which was terrifying. When I arrived, I saw that my sister was there, too. Any time I was called to his office, I had the strangest mixture of pleasure that he had noticed me and utter dread that I was about to be punished for something I didn't even know I did wrong. Whether it would be "Well done" or "Depart from me," one could never know going in.

Pastor got right to the point: He told my sister and I that our parents were having some problems and it looked like they might be splitting up. My stomach sank, hard. He said my dad was a failure and my mom was getting to her breaking point in putting up with him. It would likely all be over soon. My heart pounded and my head swam. I will forever remember his next words to us.

"You guys can call me Dad if you want."

Once those words left Pastor's mouth, my ears started ringing. I could see that he continued to talk, but I had no idea what he was saying. In a daze, I walked out of that meeting experiencing an odd blend of privilege and intense confusion. Pastor was looking out for me, and I trusted him. I didn't feel like I could trust my parents anymore. And yet...didn't Pastor seem sort of happy that my parents were separating?

It turns out, neither of my parents had any idea that Pastor called this meeting with my sister and me. What's more: They had no intention of splitting up. But my parents never discussed their marriage with us, so I believed every word Pastor said.

At this point, I was in complete emotional darkness. The spiritually abusive environment I grew up in had wreaked havoc on my nervous system. I was out of control, which is something I now recognize as one of my deepest fears. My life revolved around pleasing God, and how pleased God was could be measured by how well things were going in life. Since I measured my spiritual life by how things were going with me, it didn't look good. The disintegration of my family and my own mental health could mean only one thing: God wasn't pleased with us.

As I sat alone in my room one night, I hit a new low. I had been crying and journaling for hours. I was so overwhelmed with so many emotions that, without even thinking, I dug my fingernails into my wrist as deep as I could, pulling them up my forearm. Thick red lines materialized on my skin, followed by a flash of pain. All of a sudden, I grew very calm. I stared at my arm as little prickles of blood started to appear, and I realized I felt better. I felt completely in control, much as I had when I restricted my food intake. And I had found something I could hide. Self-harm entered my life quietly yet boldly, affirming every lie I already believed. It waited quietly in the shadows while I was feeling particularly righteous. But if I believed even slightly, even for a moment, that I was doing something wrong, my mind screamed that I was worthless and deserved as much pain as I could tolerate. It was incredibly convincing. I started to hide sharp objects in several locations around my room, along with my journal, tucked away under the mattress.

As one can probably imagine, I was not able to hide everything forever. Eventually, all the messy, out-of-control parts of my life came to a head. I came home one night to my mom waiting for me, my journal in her hand. She had suspected something was very wrong and searched my room. I was horrified. I couldn't speak for days, even as my mom sat with me, desperate to know everything. I had been so conditioned by fear that I was convinced people would discard me for wasting my so-called perfect life. I wouldn't talk, because I felt like I *couldn't* talk. I was so ashamed and embarrassed about what I had been doing.

It took months after the intervention from my mom before I reached the day all the ugly things came falling out of my mouth. I was performing with the New Life Singers at a Christian school, and I was slated to share my testimony, as I had done hundreds of times before. But I was raw. I just couldn't put on my best church-kid face and talk about how good everything was with Jesus in my life. Instead, I broke down. I told a room of three hundred fellow church kids that I was a complete mess. I hated myself, and I was drowning in a sea of disorder that I hadn't even realized I could climb out of yet. I knew God was real. I wanted to believe He had begun the slow process of my healing. But I was through pretending I had it all together. I didn't have the courage to publicly name my disorders, but I was as honest as I could be at the time. To my utter surprise, the altar flooded with kids. A couple dozen of them lined up to talk to me after the performance, and they all said, "Me, too."

It was the first of many times I would find the courage to speak the truth and be met with love, compassion, and empathy. I couldn't believe how many people identified with what I was going through. I wasn't in control, but I wasn't alone either.

7

FALLING IN LOVE

THROUGH THE DARKNESS of my teenage years, another significant person was by my side: Mike. I met my soulmate and best friend when I was fourteen years old, and he supported me as fully as he possibly could through each storm I faced. Mike seemed to know the true me, and he loved me. He loved me before *I* loved me.

Our love story is its own complex, turbulent experience because of the abuses of Freedom Village. Our dating years were so unbelievably hard that if we hadn't had a firm foundation of genuine friendship beneath us, we would have never made it to our wedding day.

I first met Mike at the beginning of a weekly practice for the New Life Singers. At these hourlong practices, we would learn new music and practice for upcoming tours. Everyone in the group besides me was a program kid, and their faces would continually change. Singers were replaced if they were kicked out of New Life as a punishment within the program or if they left Freedom Village altogether. Mike was the newest replacement in the group.

Those days, I had my share of crushes on boys in New Life, because those were the people I spent most of my time with. Pastor didn't have a specific rule against staff kids being in relationships with program kids, but everyone knew that boyfriends and girlfriends were not allowed within the same singing group. This kept most relationships at the crush stage because if you did end up dating, one person would be moved to one of the other two touring musical groups. God forbid, or perhaps just Pastor forbid, Freedom Village send out vanloads of teenage lovebirds focused on each other instead of on their mission.

An unknown seventeen-year-old walked into the practice room. Sarah directed our attention to him. "Everyone, welcome Mike! He's the newest member of New Life," she said.

I took a look at him. I had seen this boy on campus recently, although I had been sure his name was Matt. He caught my attention because he had a little blond spot in the midst of his brown hair—the result of a birthmark without pigment. After coming to Freedom Village, Mike knelt at the altar one night and stopped running from God. He made progress in the program and rose through the Levels System quickly. I clapped along with everyone else, welcoming not-Matt into New Life, not suspecting that he would become the most important person in my life.

As we began to tour together, I realized that Mike was insanely cool. He had two traits that I didn't possess: He was authentic, and he didn't care what others thought of him. I fell a little bit in love with him in a church lobby where we had just performed on tour. We were waiting to shake hands with churchgoers as they left the sanctuary. Mike stood next to me, and he suddenly leaned in to whisper in my ear.

"You might want to move over, because I farted and it really stinks," he warned.

Instead of being grossed out, I thought it was so attractive how he couldn't care less about what I or anyone else thought about him. He showed a freedom from the fear of what others think that I could hardly imagine. I had been paranoid, embarrassed, and insecure for years. How could I not be interested in this guy who never seemed insecure? It didn't take long for us to become close.

As part of the New Life performances, I heard Mike's testimony over and over again. He had come into the program at Freedom Village because he was addicted to drugs. His life story was so very unlike my own. As I got to know him better, I understood the reasons for his life derailing at such a young age. I also learned that he was hilarious and fearless. He would do anything, and I mean absolutely anything, anyone dared him to do. If he wants to do something, he will do it. Mike is a guy who does the things that need to be done. He doesn't want or need to be noticed, and he doesn't go looking for people's approval—the exact opposite of how I was living when I met him. The more time I spent with Mike, the more I saw someone who possessed qualities that I didn't even know I needed.

Each time we piled into our twelve-passenger van for a tour, I claimed my seat for the trip in the second-row window seat. Mike always sat in the third-row window seat, directly behind me. I loved that he sat there! I set my pillow against the window and sat sideways, folding my legs up to my chest. Mike leaned forward, crossing his arms on the back of my seat, and we talked every minute of every drive. We both claimed we couldn't sleep on car rides, so on long trips when everyone else was sleeping, we would stay awake talking and laughing ourselves into hysterics. So many times we laughed until tears streamed down our cheeks as we tried to be quiet and avoid waking anyone else, lest they try to get in on our good time. We joked that we had a special wavelength only the two of us were on. Everyone knew we were best friends.

Mike remained a constant in my life, and we continued to

grow closer. We listened to each other share our testimonies in countless schools, churches, jails, and detention centers. I saw him pray with inmates and addicts who identified with his story, and he watched me as I prayed with church kids who had heard my own story of being a church kid. I was fifteen when I started to notice that I liked Mike as more than a friend. I was thinking about him all the time. It was obvious to both of us that we really liked each other, but we also knew that dating meant one of us would be forced to leave New Life. Not touring together felt like the worst possible scenario. So we simply enjoyed this rare Freedom Village loophole we had found, allowing us to be best friends who could spend a ton of time together. We joked that our friendship label was "It's Complicated," intentionally keeping a delicate balance between best friends and completely head over heels. It was a confusing time: I knew I loved him, and I was *pretty sure* he loved me. But I was also afraid that if I told him I loved him, he might say he saw me as a little sister, and then I'd have to just go jump off a cliff.

For a few years, everyone in leadership at Freedom Village seemed content with me and Mike being friends. Sarah, our director and my big sister, could see—as I'm sure everyone else did—that we were madly in love, but she did *not* want one of us to have to leave her group. I was New Life's lead singer, and Mike was a strong vocalist who could sing tenor, bass, or any part in between. Cringey as it is to say, Mike also had a valuable testimony: His sensationally sinful past made him a touring and fundraising commodity. Because Sarah didn't want to lose either of us, it became an unspoken rule to keep us in a state of "just friends" for as long as possible.

Mike wasn't just my best friend. He also became a part of my family. My parents often threw parties for the singing groups. Mike's attendance at these events turned into him coming over almost every weekend for dinner, and we would hang out all day and evening. These years were arguably the best for us, because we spent so much time together. But they were also torturous for me. I worried we would never get out of the dreaded friend zone.

Mike completed his Freedom Village program at eighteen, but he decided to stay indefinitely and work as staff. Nearly *every* teen who completed the program did the same thing. By the time I turned seventeen, Mike had reached the level of Junior Staff and was training to be a dean in the boys dorm. Serving as a dean was an elevated position and was considered a huge honor, because they worked one-on-one with the program kids the most. Mike had a huge heart for the boys in the dorm, along with a growing list of responsibilities. At the same time, he continued to fly under the radar, always doing what needed to be done without sucking up or trying to earn validation from Pastor. He spent time working as Freedom Village "security," which meant patrolling the campus. This fact probably wouldn't have even stuck in my mind except for the consequences it had when I began to take heat from Pastor for my alleged behavior. I'll never forget the humiliation of hauling wood with Mike on campus security duty the first night of my first No Level punishment—and many nights after that. I had to be seen by the boy I loved more than anything as I was publicly shamed, walking in circles, carrying my log.

Mike had dropped out of high school before coming into the program, so he began four years of school again at seventeen. Despite our age difference then, Mike was on track to graduate the high school education program at Freedom Village just a year before me.

Every year, our high school seniors would have a special senior banquet—what Freedom Village hosted in lieu of a traditional prom. It was a big deal because it was the one night that girls and guys could interact with one another on campus.

When Mike was a senior, he was miraculously allowed to take me—only in my junior year of high school—as his just-friends date to the senior banquet. He had also gotten permission to come to my house afterward to hang out before going back to his dorm. I was beyond thrilled. I found the most beautiful light-green dress, and I had my hair styled professionally. Mike and I went to the banquet and had the time of our lives. It was a beautiful early summer evening, and we were riding high from the perfection of our time together. When we got back to my house, the two of us decided to sit out front on my porch. This was something we often did on the weekends. My house had a great porch, with rocking chairs and a swinging seat, facing the quiet road we lived on. With my family inside the house, we sat in separate rocking chairs, just talking and finishing out a very special night.

The next morning, all Hell broke loose. When I arrived at school, my life flipped upside-down. The night before, a Freedom Village staffer had driven by and seen Mike and me sitting together on the front porch. They immediately went to Pastor to tell him we had been alone and unsupervised. Whether they shared any scandalous untruths beyond that, I never found out. No one ever spoke to me, to Mike, or to my parents to ask for details or share the accusation. By the next morning, Pastor had issued orders that went in for the kill: Mike and I were both kicked out of the New Life Singers until further notice. We weren't allowed to be friends. We weren't even allowed to speak to each other anymore. I was beyond crushed and so confused.

The cherry on top was that the day all of this happened was supposed to be an even more special day than the senior banquet. It was Mike's birthday and also his high school graduation day. I woke up excited to see my best friend, to wish him a happy birthday and give him the gifts I had bought. Instead, I was informed that I couldn't talk to or be friends with Mike, and we'd lost New Life as well. At his graduation, we both had to sit through the ceremony and watch the singing groups—*our* singing group—perform without us.

This news struck at the same time my eating disorder, shame, anxiety, and depression were already crushing me. My psyche was taking hit after hit, and I was powerless to stop it.

In case it wasn't already clear, Freedom Village's culture was destructive and suspicious. Our loss of privileges after the senior banquet was a perfect example of how it operated. Not only did we live in fear of Pastor and his array of punishments, which apparently swung with his moods, but we also mistrusted the staff members who appeared to live to catch people breaking rules so they could report it to Pastor. For every staff person who worked at Freedom Village to help others, there was another kind of staff person who seemed to enjoy their work in the ministry for very different reasons. Pastor encouraged such behavior by literally rewarding those who shared gossip and rumors. It served to increase the fear and paranoia for those of us who preferred to fly under the radar or who desperately wanted to go unnoticed by Pastor. For that matter, even the program kids who did not fall into that camp were unfairly affected by such a culture. I became incredibly adept at reading other people's moods; and no wonder, as it was a matter of my survival. I inhabited a never-ending state of over-analyzing everyone around me so that I could manipulate the situation, please anyone who needed pleasing, and stay safe.

Enduring in such a tenuous situation wasn't easy for anyone, I'm sure, but the inconsistency seemed to make it much more difficult than if we had had rigid and definitive rules to follow. Pastor would often come down hard on someone and then, by the next day, experience a change in mood and reverse their punishment. And so it was, as another New Life tour approached and our talents were needed, Mike and I were given our privileges back so we could reclaim our places in the singing group. Our heads spun at the punishment and subsequent revocation, though it wasn't all that surprising. I was even grateful to Pastor for giving us our lives back. But we had learned a valuable lesson: We were always being watched.

That following summer was a blur as Mike buried himself in his work as a new employee of Freedom Village. I went to Ballet Magnificat for a month as usual, and I was on the precipice of making big life decisions about what I wanted to do after high school. As I approached my senior year, I needed to choose which path I was going to follow: dancing or singing. Throughout my teenage years, I had considered leaving Freedom Village after graduation—with Pastor's blessing, of course—to pursue dancing professionally with Ballet Magnificat. Dancing was a major passion of mine before my eating disorders arose. A life of doing nothing but dancing seemed like a dream come true for me. If I did leave the ministry I'd grown up in, it felt like a safe option to join the Christian ballet company because it meant I would still be in full-time Christian service. God would still be happy with me, I believed. If I wanted a life as a professional singer, it would mean staying with the New Life Singers to continue touring—and it held the possibility of pursuing a deeper relationship with Mike. That alone added whole other layers of complication to my decision. Our friendship was still officially platonic, despite the depths of my feelings for Mike. And I knew he and I were on Pastor's radar after the senior banquet incident—not in a good way.

I prayed about these decisions so much; I just wanted to do whatever it was God wanted me to do. I sought God fiercely through my emotional chaos, probably because I feared making the wrong decision and being out of His will. In fall 2004, I prepared to audition for Ballet Magnificat, even though I was beginning to get burned out on ballet. My eating disorder was rearing its ugly head, and I was relentlessly critical of my body. Just getting through ballet classes was becoming increasingly hard, mentally and physically. Dancing was stealing my joy rather than bringing me joy. Without joy, it is next to impossible to keep dancing at the level it takes to be a professional.

That October, I believe God answered my prayers about my future when New Life had a singing trip to North Carolina. We were performing in a church, and I stood on the stage watching people respond to our message and come forward to kneel at the altar. I felt what I now describe as a deep knowing: This is what I wanted to do. I had such clarity. I would cancel my dance audition, I would stay at Freedom Village, and I would sing.

Mike, certainly, was happy with my decision. During the years of our friendship, it had tortured him to know that half my heart was with dancing, which meant I might move to Mississippi for ballet. Now, we knew our paths were aligned.

One Wednesday soon after, I was home from school with a ballet-related back injury. Over lunch, one of my staff kid friends came to my house bursting with news. She said rumors were circulating around campus that Mike was going to ask for Talking Permission with me. This would mean going up on stage after the mandatory morning chapel service and getting down on one knee in front of Pastor. He would ask Pastor for his blessing on us to talk for half an hour each day. I was ecstatic that my wildest hopes and dreams were going to come true. It didn't strike me at the time how absurd it was for Mike and me to get Talking Permission after we had been best friends for three years, longer than any couple had even dated at Freedom Village. We certainly knew each other well enough. Yet I was thrilled at the thought of finally being *us*, together. We could finally be a couple.

Little did I know, it was an assurance from Pastor that spurred Mike to action. Everyone at Freedom Village knew Mike and I were in love and, apparently, that included Pastor. I had not pressed the issue of dating because I was sure he would never give us his blessing. After all, we were a powerhouse combination for fundraising in the New Life Singers; if we dated, we'd be separated on tour, and that could affect the ministry's bottom line.

Pastor had a weekly radio show and television show, both called *Victory Today*. During the show, Pastor preached as well as interviewed a program kid, who would share their testimony, interview style, with Pastor. In late October 2004, Mike was the featured troubled teen sharing his testimony on the TV program. When filming finished, Pastor unexpectedly began questioning Mike about our relationship.

"Don't you and Mary Siegfried like each other?" Pastor asked.

Mike was completely caught off-guard.

"Yes," he said cautiously, not trusting Pastor's motive for asking.

"Well, why don't you ask for Talking Permission with her?" Pastor replied, as if such a thing was a simple, easy feat.

Mike carefully considered his next words. Pastor was known for leading people into verbal traps, and whatever he said could and would be used against us in the court of Freedom Village. He told Pastor that he hadn't asked for Talking Permission because neither of us wanted to be taken out of the New Life Singers. Pastor assured Mike that he could ask for Talking Permission the next morning at chapel and he would not remove either of us from New Life. Mike's head was swimming.

The news traveled throughout Freedom Village quickly. Although it wasn't required for Mike to ask my parents for their blessing to date me—the only person who decided whether we could date was Pastor—he sought out my dad anyway. By the time Mike went to the administration building my dad worked in, my father already knew why he was there. He met Mike in the lobby, laid hands on his shoulders, and said, "You've got my blessing."

When my parents came home from church that night, I could tell by the looks on their faces that the rumor was true.

"I think someone is going to call you tonight. You might want to sit by the phone!" they said.

So I camped out at the top of the stairs with our landline phone in hand and waited. It had been several long years of liking Mike but feeling certain we could never be together. Yet I knew in my heart that it had to be Mike. It was always Mike. The phone rang. My hands were sweaty and shaky as I answered it and heard Mike's voice on the other end. He asked me if I wanted to make this official, saying he was going to "take the knee" in chapel the next morning to ask for Talking Permission. I was overjoyed.

Mike and I often talk about how, from that moment on, that was *it* for us. We might as well have gotten married after he called me, because from that night forward, neither of us had a shred of doubt that we would be together for life.

I feel lucky and, honestly, a little weird to have loved only one man and had only one real relationship. I knew a lot of church kids who grew up like me and married the only person they had ever dated because, it seemed to me, there weren't a lot of options around. I know in my heart that there was and is no other man on Earth I could have possibly been meant for. Sure, I could have ended up with someone else. But God saw fit to bring Mike into my life when I needed a friend with no ulterior motives, someone who knew me as I grew up and who could understand my life at Freedom Village.

The day Mike called me, we knew we had permission to be together. What we didn't know was how much we would suffer as a couple while dating at Freedom Village. God had given us a solid foundation of deep friendship and ministry together in order to prepare us for what we were about to endure at the hands of Pastor and his staff cronies. Our level of friendship mirrored my parents' love, and I'm sure that Pastor hated us for it. We knew each other inside and out. And it was a good thing we did. Life was about to get very difficult for both of us, but having love as our foundation would be our saving grace.

8

HARD LOVE

WITHIN THE UNUSUAL bubble of our friendship, Mike and I were relatively safe. Once we officially became a couple, attacks on our relationship became intense. I call our love a hard love. To me, hard love is real life. You skip along together during the sweet times, but you fight for—and with—each other when you're in the trenches.

The culture and structure of Freedom Village was massively destructive to personal relationships, especially among the staff. It was almost impossible to have healthy long-term relationships. Anytime a beautiful connection started to take shape, it was attacked systematically until it was broken down. I watched this happen over and over with both friendships and romantic relationships.

In our family in particular, Pastor took efforts to ruin every romantic relationship. He didn't stop at meddling in my mom and dad's marriage. Sarah, who dated Pastor's son for many years, didn't seem to get the full force of abuse from Pastor. In many ways, it seemed like my sister was the most favored Siegfried child in Freedom Village. But when Sarah and Pastor's son were no longer dating, Pastor specifically counseled Sarah to pursue a relationship that my parents didn't condone, driving a wedge between a daughter and her parents. That relationship ended painfully. My sister moved on and eventually dated someone new. *Their* relationship flourished, and they got engaged in 2006. The night before Pastor married Sarah and her husband, he made a *huge* deal about a picture of the two of them kissing that appeared in the slideshow they planned to show at their wedding. This was despite the fact that they were both in their late twenties and that he had actually given them permission to kiss. Pastor also forbade my brother to date a girl who lived out of state, even though my parents approved of them dating. It caused a lot of pain in our family, and my brother's relationship ultimately ended. The same things might have happened without Pastor's meddling, but it certainly didn't help.

One of the greatest challenges for me and Mike fell into place the moment we became a couple. We received Talking Permission from Pastor—but, ironically, it dragged us backward in our relationship. Where we had once been virtually inseparable, with Talking Permission, we were restricted to seeing each other for only thirty minutes a day in the loud, crowded cafeteria at lunchtime. Where Mike had previously come to my house nearly every weekend to hang out and have dinner with my family, he was now never allowed to visit.

Worst of all, we quickly realized that Pastor had lied about allowing us to continue to tour the country together with the New Life Singers. Mike was moved into the Victory Singers the week we got Talking Permission. When I showed up at our usual weekly practice, I realized how awful singing was going to be without Mike. I sat on the floor, singing barely above a whisper and crying through the entire practice. This was my first love, my first boyfriend, and it was already far harder than I imagined it could be.

For couples with Talking Permission, any contact outside of lunch was forbidden. When we saw each other in the hallway, we had to avert our eyes and keep walking. If we didn't, or if we took a moment to stop and chat, someone would pull one or both of us aside to yell at us. That was the best-case scenario: they might skip the yelling and go straight to telling Pastor that we were being sneaky and talking. We were so in love, and so paranoid.

I've noted before that the rules for relationships were vastly different for Pastor than for everyone else. But even more confusing were the standards of dating for staff kids. Pastor was known for changing rules and having favorites. Double standards and shifting expectations made it hard to know what your own rules were on any given day. My sister Sarah and Pastor's son had been a dream couple before they broke things off. They had powerhouse vocals and would sing moving duets in church. As a couple, they didn't have to adhere to the established rules of Freedom Village, like the Six-Inch Rule and around-the-clock accountability with chaperones. No males and females were allowed to be alone together unless they were married—unless you were Pastor, his son, or someone in his good graces apparently. I got the impression that Sarah was able to live her life in a more Pastor-pleasing way than I could ever figure out.

Pastor had created a kingdom of haves and have-nots, and he seemed to enjoy sowing discord among us. If Pastor wanted two people to begin a romantic relationship, he would make it happen —not to champion anyone's love but to rearrange the game board. Mike and I weren't among the couples who were allowed to live above the rules. No, Pastor personally tried to destroy our love.

When I started to date Mike, Pastor seemed very interested in and involved with our relationship. Sometimes he championed us and the rules were relaxed. Other times, he stood clearly against us. It was hard to keep up with the inconsistencies.

Perhaps his fascination had to do with me specifically. I sensed that Pastor didn't quite *get* me. Sometimes I could feel him watching me—not necessarily in a creepy way, but as if he were trying to figure out what was going on in my head. Pastor would say that to me, actually: that he never really knew what I was thinking. Maybe that was my superpower. If he tried to start a conversation with me, I gave the shortest answers possible. I shrank into myself, pretending I wasn't there, and denied him the chance to get to know me. I was mightily afraid of Pastor, though I didn't hate him. I fully believed he was a man of God, to be respected above anyone else. It never occurred to me to question him or his authority, because he was sent by God to rule over my life. But I was utterly terrified of him. Let me be clear that I am not exaggerating: I was *terrified* of Pastor.

Eventually, maybe because we had no other choice, Mike and I got used to our new normal: spending virtually no time together, having no ability to communicate as we had before, and getting punished when we tried to communicate at unapproved times. Instead, we tried to enjoy the fact that we had conquered the first hurdle of being a couple.

On Valentine's Day, I came home from school to a big bouquet of red roses and a letter. Mike had received permission from Pastor to take me on a date that night to a fancy restaurant, chaperoned by my parents. He wrote about how much I meant to him, how he had prayed every day that we would be able to be a couple, and that he was so thankful God answered those prayers. At the end of the three-page letter, Mike told me he loved me for the first time. My heart exploded! It was so meaningful to read his words and know that he was mine.

I was floating on a cloud during our date. My parents let us sit at a table by ourselves, even though they were supposed to be on us like glue. Over dinner, Mike shared even more good news: He had asked Pastor for Dating Permission, which had been granted without his taking the knee in church. We had successfully moved up to the next level. As we got into the car to leave the restaurant, Mike and I held hands for the first time. I thought I was going to die of happiness. He held my hand like he would never let go, all the way home.

When we said goodbye, Mike looked at me with a sappy, lovesick smile on his face. "I love you," he said.

"I love you," I replied, the first of a million times I would exchange those words with him.

DATING PERMISSION, intended for serious couples who had already gotten to know each other, meant Mike and I could have one date a week. But this level had even more blurry and inconsistent rules than Talking Permission did. While it was clear that program kids could not touch or be alone together even with Dating Permission, the rules for staff kids seemed to be more relaxed. That is, until Mike and I reached that level.

All of a sudden, Pastor came down hard on all staff and program couples. I know it's common for teenagers to presume that everyone is out to get them, but it really felt as if Pastor always changed the rules or made them harder to follow once I was of age to obey them. Pastor announced that staff parents could no longer determine their own children's dating rules. The dating rules that had previously applied only to those in the program were now universal rules at Freedom Village.

This structure was drastically at odds with the depth of our relationship. Once people started dating at Freedom Village, it was as if it was a sin to love each other. Sit too close to each other and be reprimanded. Talk a little too long in passing and be told you were taking your focus off God and making your relationship an idol. Mike and I were allowed to spend our date each week hanging out at my house, and we were permitted to write letters to each other. We relied on those letters, writing nearly every day. Mike would give me a note before I went to school, and it would get me through whatever confusing scenario we were facing that day. Pastor continued to be involved in our relationship and would attack if one of us made a mistake. As a couple, we became even more acquainted with the ebb and flow of Pastor's moods. Obedience really did bring blessings. If we followed Pastor's every word, no matter how inconsistent, he would bless us, such as by giving us permission for a hug.

Mike soon became Senior Staff, the highest level at Freedom Village, and a dean in the boys dorm. He worked closely with the nearly one hundred boys in the program. His jobs as a counselor and a residence assistant came with duties like mailing out the program boys' letters home. Uncharacteristically, there came a day Mike was late mailing out the letters. When Pastor heard, he swiftly and harshly punished him. Pastor stripped Mike of his position as dean and put him in charge of cleaning the dump.

The dump was an area on campus where we kept two or three dumpsters for everyone's trash. I was told that the ministry was too poor to regularly pay for a disposal service to come pick up the trash. As you can imagine, the trash bags would overflow, get ripped apart by animals, and bake all day in the sun. It was a nasty place.

Pastor also took away our Dating Permission for ten weeks. It meant we couldn't so much as look at each other, let alone talk. Instead, I had to watch the hardworking man I loved clean the dump every day for months.

To put it in perspective, this coincided with the meeting when Pastor told me and Sarah that we could call him Dad because my parents were inevitably getting divorced. I was shattered by the reduction in our relationship privileges at a time when I was already emotionally vulnerable. And yet, I wasn't even mad at Pastor. I blamed myself. I had fallen too hard for Mike, and God was punishing us for putting each other before Him. Or perhaps Mike's punishment from Pastor was really God punishing me for having an eating disorder and being a hypocrite, and Mike was paying the price for my sin. Freedom Village had conditioned me, through brainwashing and disordered thinking, to see anything going wrong in my life as the result of God's disappointment with me. When "hard" was synonymous with "bad," life became something I was unprepared for and unable to handle. After all, disobedience brings consequences.

I continued to write letters to Mike every day, counting down the ten weeks until I could give him the collection of notes. I didn't know it, but Mike was doing the same thing. One day, I found flowers on my desk at school; he had picked them at the dump and put them there to brighten up my day. I didn't tell anyone the flowers were from Mike because I was afraid. But in that glimmer through the fog, I knew this man was my soulmate. We were taking the hits together, and we were going to make it through. God was with us. God was for us.

In a bold move, Mike asked Pastor to restore our Dating Permission in time for my birthday, which fell before the end of the ten weeks. Mike told me that when he approached Pastor, it was as if he had forgotten he had taken Dating Permission away from us in the first place. I'm sure he had. It seemed he had no idea the Hell he was making us live day by day—but still we were so grateful to Pastor for restoring our *us* to us.

Occasionally, Mike would bring me the news that he had

asked permission to give me one hug, and Pastor had granted it. Taking full advantage of our one hug, Mike and I wrapped our arms around each other and stayed that way for fifteen minutes. Within those embraces, I felt we were safe as a couple. While I was in Mike's arms, I knew we could endure whatever it took to make it to marriage, when no one could touch us anymore.

I graduated from high school that spring and decided I wanted to work in the department that organized and booked the tours for the Victory Singers, Sounds of Freedom, and the New Life Singers. One of these groups was out on tour nearly every week, so it would be a busy job. I got my own office, decorated it just how I wanted it, and started work that summer. I also headed off for my last summer intensive at Ballet Magnificat, where I would stay for four weeks. Mike saw me off with another long, Pastor-approved hug, and we promised to write letters and call each other every day after I arrived in Mississippi.

I had been there for nearly a week when my mom called. Someone I had trusted told Pastor that Mike and I were breaking the rules of Dating Permission with our hugs and—I'm not really clear on this point—being in love too much? It was as if Pastor forgot that he had given us permission for every single hug we shared, for every single moment we spent together. He was making the rules for dating even more strict, and he was making an example out of me and Mike.

Pastor took our Dating Permission away indefinitely, ending our relationship.

I tried to process this news while sitting alone on my bed in a dorm room thousands of miles from anyone who could remotely understand my life. My roommate asked what was wrong, but even as I tried to explain it, I knew she wouldn't get it. I cried all night, unable to even call Mike to say goodbye. Essentially, I had been in an abusive three-way relationship, and now it was over.

The rest of my time in Mississippi passed in a fog as I prayed, asking God what I had done wrong. Something bad had happened to me, which had to have been the result of my sin and disobedience—but I also knew that loving Mike was *not* a sin. The confusion was overwhelming. I submitted faithfully to learn whatever lesson God might have been teaching me. I believed that if my heart were in the wrong place—say, I had elevated my relationship with Mike above my relationship with God—that He would allow bad things to happen to me to help put my focus back on Him. My job was to submit. No complaining. No lamenting. No questioning. I needed to yield to my circumstances so that I could get back into the "right standing" with God. Oh, how I wish I would have realized that this God I knew sounded so...human.

I came home at the end of the summer hoping it was all a bad dream or that Mike had once again convinced Pastor to let us date, like he had for my birthday. Maybe Mike would even show up at the airport with my parents to pick me up as a surprise. No such luck. When I did catch a glimpse of Mike after getting home, all I could see was the pain in his eyes. One of the few good things in my world had been shattered, and I sunk deeper into depression.

Everyone at Freedom Village knew everything about Pastor taking away our Dating Permission. The shame and embarrassment of my fall from grace threatened to suffocate me. Our community was full of people happy to see one another's failures and punishments—probably because it meant, for that moment, you weren't the one in Pastor's bull's-eye.

In fall 2005, I was eighteen and getting settled into working with my sister in the tour-booking department for the singing groups. I was in my new office one day when I got a call from a teacher in the program girls' school room, asking if I would be willing to help because they were short-staffed that day. I'd planned to never see that classroom again after I graduated, but I went downstairs to help—and I never went back to my office. It was decided for me that I would work in the school. I was a great teacher for the program girls' classroom because I had followed the same curriculum from kindergarten through twelfth grade. I didn't want to teach school. But of course, I agreed to do it.

About a month into my new job as a teacher, the school principal called me into a meeting. Unsolicited, he told me he hoped I would work on being more assertive. "Okay," I thought, unsure of how I would proceed with that advice. As I walked out of that meeting, Pastor barreled down the hallway toward me.

"WELL, MARY!" he boomed as he grabbed me and wrapped me in a big bear hug. "HOW ARE YOU?"

Looking back, I wonder whether Pastor was half-drunk and feeling on top of the world. Pushing away how unbelievable it was that Pastor could be so oblivious to the pain he had caused me, I jumped on the moment. I knew he was happy with me right then. I would be more assertive.

"Can Mike and I have our Dating Permission back?" I squeaked out.

For a moment, I watched the gears turn as he tried to recall what I was talking about. It was just the way Mike had described Pastor when he'd asked for our Talking Permission back. I was sure he didn't even remember taking it away from us.

"I think that would be all right," Pastor finally responded.

I shrugged out from under Pastor's huge arm, still wrapped around me, told him how thankful I was, and quickly walked away. I ran to the cafeteria, where I knew Mike would be monitoring the program boys' lunch. I walked right up to him, his face a picture of terror, then confusion, as I seemed to break the rules. I told Mike what I had done, and sheer joy spread across his features. We were *us* again.

We were thrilled to be back together, but the out-of-our-control, on-again-off-again nature of our relationship was still taking a toll on us. I was falling apart. Mike was the first person I talked to about my disordered eating. I eventually opened up about the self-harm too. I remember Mike asking me to show him the marks on my arm, then just holding me like I was a fragile glass object. I *was* fragile, and I was terrified of opening up to anyone, even Mike. At Freedom Village, vulnerability and intimacy were punished.

After my mom found my journal, I started the slow process of healing, and Mike was there through it all. He became my steady rock, the constant among my peers. One of my favorite things about Mike, as I understand him today, is his radical acceptance of people. His acceptance of me drew me to him, even when I didn't really know who I was and lived in fear of myself. He supported me by loving me for who I was then and who I would become.

Because of the paranoid atmosphere of Freedom Village, we never had a lot of time to discuss things at length. Gone were the days of talking for twelve hours straight in the van on our singing trips. We had a three-hour date each week, but we otherwise weren't supposed to hang out or talk too much. If we did try to communicate, we'd get reported, and considering everything we had been through so far, neither of us wanted to risk punishment again. During a disagreement or a moment of stress for either of us, we could never address it head-on. When it came time for a date, we just wanted to enjoy our rare time together. The circumstances made communication hard. So many times, I would need to talk to Mike on campus during the day, but I could see the fear of repercussions in his eyes, and no doubt he saw the same fear in mine. Communication, the greatest need in any relationship, was our biggest threat. In a cruel twist, Mike was the one person I was comfortable opening up to but I wasn't allowed to. It created (or furthered) habits that I'm still unlearning years later: burying problems and avoiding confrontation.

In the spring of 2006, I was doing a little bit better. My parents had practically banned both sharp objects and journals from my life. If I started to write a poem, inspiration would dry up. It was as if my gift for writing was gone. It also became clear that I needed to stop dancing. Once I let the seed of self-hatred in, I couldn't stand being in a studio. Just as I would think I was beginning to heal from my eating disorders, it would come time to put on a leotard and tights and stand in front of a mirror for hours. I had no confidence in my dancing any longer, and I was burned out. After I danced my last performance that spring, I threw everything related to ballet in the trash.

I felt like God was stripping me down to my heart alone. I didn't tour and sing with Mike anymore. I wasn't allowed to journal, and I couldn't come up with even a short poem. I had given up dancing after a lifetime of ballet. Although I did have Mike, in reality, our relationship was always on the verge of being taken away.

Because of the rules, Mike and I hardly ever touched each other, and I had never kissed anyone. I wasn't a girl who wanted her first kiss to be at the altar on her wedding day, which was well within the realm of possibility at Freedom Village. I always hoped we would kiss—with Pastor's approval, of course—for the first time when Mike and I got engaged. There was a chance Pastor would give us permission then, if he was in a good mood.

On my nineteenth birthday, Mike came over to my house for a date. Even though my parents were always home to chaperone us, they gave us space instead of staring at us and making it uncomfortable. I believe they trusted us. I was a well-behaved kid who avoided mistakes at all costs, so I don't think they laid awake worrying at night about whether Mike and I were sleeping together. After all, I loved blessings and feared consequences.

Mike had gotten permission from Pastor for us to hug that day. As we hugged our approved hug in the relative privacy of my living room, we fell into a kiss before either of us fully realized it was happening. It was tender and wonderful, and I was so happy I had waited for that first kiss to be with Mike.

We crossed a glorious milestone three months later. My sister and her husband chaperoned us to a nearby gorge with beautiful waterfalls and hiking paths. Mike and I hiked to a little clearing overlooking the water. I suddenly realized that our chaperones were gone. I turned around to see Mike on one knee. I don't remember what he said, because the only thought racing through my mind was *"It's happening!"* Mike and I were engaged, and the countdown to being inseparable began.

It should have been no surprise that the Freedom Village rules for engaged couples were inconsistent and inconsistently applied. The unspoken rule was that once you were engaged, the strict code of conduct for relationships became more relaxed. This could mean different things for different people: Some couples could kiss as long as it wasn't in front of program kids, and some couples were allowed to drive in a car alone. Nothing was explained clearly though, and no one dared ask for clarification in case the rules became even stricter; everyone kind of kept their heads down and hoped for the best. Sarah, who in her late twenties was "way old" to be getting married in church culture, had much more flexible rules for her recent engagement than Mike and I had. It was no secret that Pastor's son went around carelessly bragging about having sex before he married his wife, whereas other engaged couples were terrified to be seen holding hands. While Mike and I were engaged, we would kiss and hold hands in private, and my parents were okay with both.

My sister's wedding was at the end of that year. Pastor had just criticized them for wanting to play their slideshow, because people at Freedom Village would see evidence of a couple kissing before marriage. Sarah cried the night before and through most of her wedding day because of how vitriolic his comments had been. At the all-staff meeting the following Monday, Pastor ripped into my parents for their moral failure regarding my sister. He screamed that we had clear ministry rules stating that couples could not, under any circumstances, violate the Six-Inch Rule until they were married. My parents were gutted. The entire staff sat in judgment of my family. I looked over at Mike during that meeting, knowing that it meant we'd have to wait out our eight-month-long engagement with no more kissing, hugging, or hand-holding. Pastor seemed to be taking one more swing at me and Mike before his power over our relationship would be diminished. He knew Mike and I were a perfect match; maybe that's why he hated us.

Pastor said he would never marry a teenager, so Mike and I set our wedding date for May, two weeks after my twentieth birthday. At this point, we had been together two or three times longer than most older couples who were married at Freedom Village. On a sunny and beautiful spring day in 2007, we became Mike and Mary Rosenberger. It was, by far, the best day of my life. Pastor married us—something I'd go back and change if I could—but I was relieved that he wasn't in the mood to be awful that day.

Mike and I had made it to the relative safety of marriage. From the second we were married, everything felt completely, finally, right. Enduring all the tribulations of my teenage years bonded us. As I said, it's a hard love. Mike and I aren't a perfect couple, but the struggles have been worth every second together. As best friends and now life partners, we moved into the next stage of our life, having already overcome so much but still not knowing the challenges that lay ahead.

9

KOOL-AID

AFTER WE RETURNED from our weeklong honeymoon in Breckenridge, Colorado, Mike and I could finally spend as much time as we wanted together without fear of repercussions. Pastor didn't have the same type of control over us now that we were married—but I was naive to how our brokenness and trauma would continue to affect our relationship.

I felt as if my life as an adult had officially begun, but I was still a child in so many ways. I lived with my parents until the day I was married. I had never even kept my own bedroom clean; now I was a wife with a home to look after. Life had not offered me the opportunity to be a single adult who could learn who I was outside of the context of my relationship with Mike. I had some growing up to do.

Our first home together was a two-bedroom apartment in the boys dormitory on the Freedom Village campus. Only a hallway door separated our apartment from the program boys' living quarters. I'd often leave for work in the morning, and the hallway door would be wide open. The program boys, who rarely interacted with females, would greet me while ironing their shirts or roaming the dorm hallways. All the same, I loved that little apartment. Mike and I had fixed it up the best we could in the months before we moved in. We painted the walls, renovated the bathroom, and added homey touches. It felt so right and good to finally live together, and we entered a whole new realm of knowing each other.

I had officially moved on from being a staff kid at Freedom Village. I was on staff, an adult, and I was still drinking the Kool-Aid.

I don't use that phrase flippantly, because it has tragic roots. The leader of the Peoples Temple cult in Jonestown, Guyana, convinced more than nine hundred of his followers and their children to drink cyanide-laced punch in a 1978 massacre. It may seem an extreme comparison, but I identify with those victims. I was, in nearly every sense of the term, drinking the Kool-Aid at Freedom Village.

I was a devoted believer who accepted whatever Pastor taught me as truth; I believed that living in fear would save me. Though Pastor's teachings were supposedly based on Scripture and seemingly innocuous, in reality they were anything but. His words—infused with familiar terms such as *Jesus, gospel, sanctification,* and *holiness*—were like a sweet yet toxic drink, instilling fear and condemnation within his followers, all in the name of God. Pastor's doctrines were laced with the poison of fear; his sermons dripped with such a heavy dose of condemnation that we walked away sick and came back for more, always getting sicker.

Freedom Village did *have* a payroll, but the staff never knew *when* we were getting paid. If staff complained about the lack of regular pay, we were told our hearts weren't in the right place. Personally, I couldn't comprehend a world where employees were paid for their work every two weeks like clockwork, and I couldn't fathom that it might be unethical for an employer to refuse to pay employees. Pastor would instead constantly remind us how lucky we were to have our housing, utilities, and meals on campus paid for—these benefits would even out to a generous paycheck. If someone questioned the system, Pastor said we were ungrateful. I hadn't known that my parents had dealt with this financial instability my whole life; I never realized how poor we actually were. At times my parents couldn't buy diapers, much less make a car payment. My mom's ballet school was our only reliable source of income, which was more than most of my staff kid friends had. But even when I grew up and acknowledged the situation, none of this seemed wrong to me. I believed all along that we had lived by faith, and our lack of financial stability only served to build that faith.

Staff frequently had no money and no consistency of income, which bred an unhealthy relationship with finances. The longer staff members lived at Freedom Village, the more their ability to manage and save money, and to live in a financially responsible manner, declined. From what I saw, most of the staff lived on food stamps, none of us had good credit, and there was no point in even having a savings account, because we instantly spent whatever money we were given. Most of Freedom Village's staff had come through the program as teenagers, but the ministry didn't teach skills like personal finance or job interviewing. Instead, the emphasis was on how hard it was to make it in the outside world, which had already mistreated many of these kids. We heavy-handedly counseled program graduates who wanted to leave our community to stay in God's will (that is, to stay at Freedom Village). Pastor had built a staff of graduated program kids who were already uneasy about going back into the real world, and thus, when he told them to be grateful for what they were given, they usually were.

There wasn't a lack of funds coming into Freedom Village: parents paid tuition for the program, though it was very low; donors wrote checks both modest and generous after watching or listening to *Victory Today*; and our singing groups collected money at every show. Pastor was very good at using program kids' testimonies to solicit donations (he cleverly convinced people they were giving a tithe, or offering, to God's kingdom) to support those teenagers—but I personally didn't see most of that money going to them. While some of us on staff regularly went six weeks without receiving a single paycheck, Pastor bought new cars and took people to restaurants for steak dinners. He preached that someday, when we all had served God as long as he had, we would have these blessings too.

I believed him. Others on the staff were confused and bitter about the disparity between Pastor's situation and theirs, but Freedom Village was the only environment I'd ever known. I had a full-time job teaching, and it didn't strike me as odd that I wasn't on payroll. Mike wasn't even put on payroll until after we were married, which I thought was normal. His pay as the boys' dean was set around two hundred dollars a week for sixty- to seventy-hour workweeks—but we could never rely on Mike getting a paycheck at any consistent interval.

After three months in our dorm apartment, Mike and I were given a staff home off-campus. The ministry owned several homes in the area, and staff families would be provided with these homes to live in rent-free, with electric, water, and heating bills covered. I thought we were so lucky: free cafeteria meals, no housing bills, and no real costs of living—as long as we didn't want to take a vacation, buy a car, or eat our own food at home.

Freedom Village's abusive framework was holding strong, because I knew I was living by faith. I felt bad for employees in the outside world, who didn't have a man like Pastor to care for them.

It makes sense now that "outsiders" who joined the staff didn't usually stay long. They must have easily seen the flaws of Freedom Village: Our preacher never went to seminary, our counselors never received training, the principal and teachers (like me) never went to college, and staff couldn't even count on a paycheck. What others might see as unconventional and strange, such as my sudden recruitment from the travel booking department into the program school, triggered no suspicion for me that I might be working in an unhealthy environment.

"Your heart is desperately wicked, so you cannot trust yourself. Your authority is God, and He gave you Pastor to trust to make decisions for you." This is the framework I grew up with.

Before my first job had even gotten underway, I was told to work as a teacher's aide, a job that wasn't aligned with my interests or experience, and I did as I was instructed. In early 2008, the program girls' teacher decided to leave Freedom Village—on bad terms, of course. The principal sat me down and informed me that I would take over as the head teacher come fall. I was gobsmacked. I was only twenty, and I would be in charge of the high school education of up to seventy-five program girls between the ages of thirteen and twenty-one. Gobsmacked maybe, but not suspicious.

Our classroom was a large, open space in the basement of the building that held Freedom Village's cafeteria and chapel. Lining the walls were individual cubicles to seat each student. We used the Accelerated Christian Education curriculum, which was the same I had graduated from. ACE provided workbooks on different subjects and was common in Christian homeschooling programs. Students would teach themselves as they completed workbooks, designed to take about two weeks each. When a student completed twelve math workbooks, for example, they would earn one math credit.

Each time a teen entered the program, I gave them a diagnostic to see which grade level they tested into. Most kids tested into the fifth-grade level; they'd faced enough challenges in their personal lives that they hadn't cared about school for years. Students would also test into different levels for individual subjects, so one student might be placed into third-grade spelling, fourth-grade math, sixth-grade English, and eighth-grade social studies and science. The teens would work at their own pace on various subjects throughout the day, and the staff on duty were there to answer questions whenever a student needed help. I usually had one or two teacher's aides, and it was all up to us to help any student with any subject. That made the student-teacher ratio 75:2, and we worked with a lot of students who weren't interested in school.

I did end up enjoying teaching. One positive aspect of my training was that I did as I was told, was flexible, and found the good in it. I loved helping people understand things; I enjoyed discovering how to teach the same concept in different ways, based on how each individual student learned. I grew into a dedicated staff member with an important place in Pastor's ministry. I worked at least fifty hours a week, and if I was ever on payroll, I don't remember it.

Every Monday morning, I attended the staff meeting, the most unnerving part of the week for me and many other staff members. Pastor generally used this time to tell us how much we were failing. Nothing was ever good enough. One Monday, Pastor spent forty-five minutes ripping into the staff because visitors to the church had needed to wait a few seconds for staff people talking in the aisle to move aside. He was *livid*. Pastor's reputation was clearly what he valued the most. He prioritized the opinions of outsiders over the well-being of his own staff. Pastor called us stupid, incompetent, and sinful. He frequently wielded a phrase that was as sharp as a dagger at Freedom Village: "Your heart's not in the right place." I loved helping people and living every day for a higher purpose. The problem was that I was convinced Freedom Village was the only place someone could do that. I was genuinely grateful for this abusive environment.

Although I had grown up, in many ways I was still a scared little girl—and the longer I worked at Freedom Village, the more paranoid I became. I didn't buy a dress without wondering whether Pastor would approve. I didn't confide in a friend without some part of me wondering if they would tell Pastor my secrets. I ran any interaction with fellow staff members through an inner sounding board, attempting to figure out what Pastor thought of them, what they might tell Pastor about me, and what Pastor might tell them about me. I cared far more whether Pastor *thought* I was a hard worker than whether I actually *was* a hard worker. Pastor tainted every thought that went through my head.

I fed off the Kool-Aid of Pastor's approval. When I had that, life was good. When I didn't, all I cared about was regaining it. I feel certain that Pastor loved this dynamic. I never held him to a standard of perfection, but he constantly demanded perfection from me.

Any successful cult leader feeds their victims a steady stream of one thing: their own worst fear. *That* is the cyanide in the Kool-Aid of spiritual abuse. Fear saturates their every thought. This keeps the victim in a never-ending state of paranoia, and that paranoia feels like productive thought. I can now see that I wasn't thinking at all while I was at Freedom Village—I was mentally obsessing over fear. The ultimate fear Pastor used to control our lives is one that's central to Western Christianity: Hell.

10

THE FORBIDDEN THOUGHT

"DON'T BE surprised one day when you see my mansion in Heaven, and you get led by one of the angels to your grass shack because you didn't serve God full-time or serve him enough," Pastor preached, not for the first time. "There won't be room for some of you at the banquet feast in God's kingdom because your hearts weren't in the right place. You'll see me dining with Jesus, and *you* won't get a spot at the table because you worried too much about paychecks, or you left God's will and He took His hand off your life."

When I was a child, everything was either/or. Either you were saved or you were going to Hell. Either you were in God's favor or He would make your life difficult. Either Pastor was pleased with you or he would hand down punishments. Pastor hammered us with his message, "Obedience brings blessings; disobedience brings consequences."

Conveniently, he set the stage to have nice things himself, while those he employed went without. When he had nice things, I saw them as blessings for his obedience to God. That psychological messaging kept any questioning of Pastor at bay while he lived a different lifestyle from the rest of us. He didn't hesitate to preach about it in so many words, either. Pastor explained in an often-repeated sermon that he had nice things because he had served God for so long.

I'm sure some part of me wanted nice things, but as a newly minted "adult" in Freedom Village, I emphasized the service part above all. I always found out what was expected of me at Freedom Village, and I delivered. The next step along my path—motherhood—would be no different.

Marrying young and having a baby within a year was the norm in our community, so at twenty-one, it was time for me to get pregnant. I always knew I wanted to be a mother at some point, but unlike some of the other young women I worked alongside, I was never desperate for children. I had never babysat a day in my life. I didn't particularly connect with young children. I worked occasionally in Freedom Village's nursery, but I didn't enjoy it. I was never a baby whisperer—one of those people who could calm an infant instantly within the comfort of their magical, soothing arms. Instead, babies started to cry as soon as I held them. I was terrified this meant I was going to be a horrible mother.

Even with this thought in the back of my mind, I didn't think through the decision to get pregnant; having babies was simply what married women did. If you made it to your second year of marriage without a pregnancy announcement, people started asking questions.

So it was time to move forward and settle down. Mike and I were married adults, traveling together again with the New Life Singers. We still toured full-time, alongside our full-time jobs at Freedom Village. For the first time, as I considered motherhood, I thought about passing on the torch in our singing group and retiring from tour life. If we started having children, something would have to give. There was just one problem: There was no way I would be released from New Life. Other staff women who were lead singers had been required to keep touring *with* their kids, even if they wanted to stop. I would have to be one of those women.

Mike and I didn't tell many people when we started trying to have a baby. I daydreamed endlessly about how it would feel to take a pregnancy test and see a positive result. I had a feeling it would be both exciting and terrifying. Nearly every month between May and November I had taken a test, each time hoping that would be the time I found out we were expecting. By winter, we were in the full swing of Christmas programs. Freedom Village toured a Christmas cantata every year, involving nearly every program kid and staff member. These cantatas were a huge fundraiser for the ministry. We performed in Toronto, Canada; Buffalo, New York; and three locations in Pennsylvania. It was a massive undertaking: We loaded up buses with over a hundred singers and hauled truckloads of sound equipment, Christmas decor, and merchandise to each venue. Our set-up and tear-down systems operated like a well-oiled machine. As a dean, Mike kept track of the program boys, and I joined him in his van as he drove the teen boys and a trailer full of sound equipment to every show.

Mike and I were on our way to York, Pennsylvania, for a Christmas banquet when I realized that my period was late. Our whole giant caravan of vans and buses stopped in a Walmart parking lot for lunch, and with a hopeful heart, I snuck into the store to buy a pregnancy test. Before I returned to the van, I stuffed the test away in my bag, telling myself I'd take it the next morning after we got home. Mike drove us the rest of the way to York. As if nothing at all were different, I set up, performed, tore down, and loaded everybody back into the van.

On the way home, I started to feel cramps. My heart sank.

"What a waste to buy that pregnancy test," I thought. I felt guilty, because spending fifteen dollars on a pregnancy test was a lot of money when we never knew if or when we'd get paid.

It was the wee hours of Sunday morning before Mike and I got home. After driving all the way back, Mike was on duty to start his dorm shift at six a.m. He was back out the door before I woke up to get ready for church. No rest for the weary at Freedom Village. Despite our exhaustion, we were all expected at Sunday service that morning. There was no staying home from church, ever. Anyone who skipped a Sunday morning service would be the topic of the next staff meeting or, worse, the object of Pastor's next Sunday sermon. As I rolled out of bed, I grabbed my pregnancy test, sure that it would be another negative. I tried not to look at the test while I counted the minutes, but when I peeked at it, I saw two lines. It felt like a dream. I was pregnant!

I sat next to Mike and my family at church just a short time later, practically exploding with the news I was holding inside. But I wanted to surprise Mike, so I decided to wait until he came home from his dorm shift that afternoon. After church, I asked a friend if I could borrow her maternity jeans, the kind with a high-rise elastic top to make room for a big pregnant belly. I laid them out on our bed and waited an eternity for Mike to come home. When I told him to check out my new pair of jeans, it took a few moments for him to register what he was looking at. I showed him the positive pregnancy test just as the news hit him. We were both *so* happy. I was gripped by both nerves and excitement, like the anticipation when you are climbing the steepest hill on a roller coaster.

EVEN THOUGH WE had a baby on the way, I wasn't worried about our poverty. I had what I needed growing up, though my parents kept me blissfully ignorant of our financial insecurity. On paper, Mike and I made next to nothing, so we qualified for government-subsidized healthcare that was completely free for us. I wasn't aware that most people who worked as much as we did paid at least something for their health insurance and medical bills. I believed we were blessed to receive the tax refunds that we frugally lived off of. Mike and I (and the other staff members at Freedom Village) were truly living by faith, and we were taught that we needed to be thankful we lived this way. The circumstances made me feel like a next-level Christian: because I was in a full-time ministry, with no money or nice things, I was somehow better than other Christians. If there's any upside to having lived this way, it's that I will always appreciate any money we do have.

In the early days of our marriage, I took a calculator to the store so I could add up the cost of each item and check the total against the money I had. That tiny amount is mind-blowing now that I'm in the real world. I didn't understand that other workers' personal funds, whether for groceries, personal care, or clothing, were replenished by a regular paycheck. When Mike and I used up his two hundred dollars of "weekly" pay, the money was gone. It would be an unpredictable three or four weeks before we got another paycheck, and even then, we had to beg for it. I didn't have a clue that compensation could work differently.

The situation we faced wasn't just a lack of funds within the ministry or a lack of focus with bookkeeping though. It was Pastor's unpredictable pay schedule for staff, which added to the hostile environment. Some families did get paid every week. Those people who Pastor favored always seemed to have enough money. As I started to realize this, something new began to grow in my heart: resentment.

I left the grocery store one day, and when I reached the parking lot, a coworker from one of Pastor's favored staff families was loading so many bags of groceries into his car, they hardly fit in the trunk. I had just spent fifty dollars on the barest necessities, which Mike and I would need to stretch out for two weeks—or longer. How could he afford all these groceries and we couldn't? Mike and I primarily lived off grilled cheese and ramen noodles. If we were lucky, we got free meat that had been donated to Freedom Village, always something past the expiration date. Our poverty was so severe that we qualified for all kinds of government assistance: Supplemental Nutrition Assistance Program (SNAP), Special Supplemental Nutrition Program for Women, Infants, and Children (WIC), Low Income Home Energy Assistance Program (LIHEAP), and Medicaid. The culture I grew up in conditioned me to believe I was blessed to be living off government programs and missionary support, even while battling an intense poverty mindset. How would we survive this way as a family of three?

Common sense and fear about our finances gradually rose within me as I progressed further in my pregnancy. In my third trimester, I developed a painful urinary tract infection, common in pregnancy. Thanks to our Medicaid coverage, I was able to go to prenatal appointments, visit the doctor, and get most prescriptions without paying out of pocket. I went to Walmart to fill my script for the UTI treatment, an antibiotic, which cost only one dollar. I swiped our bank card. Denied. Completely embarrassed, I said there must be a mistake. I moved out of line to check the bank account balance over the phone. Mike and I had less than a dollar available in our account. I broke down and cried; I was humiliated that I couldn't afford medicine to heal an infection that only cost one measly dollar. Just then, I noticed Pastor's son standing there as well; he had caught sight of me crying at the store and asked me what the problem was. I had wrongly assumed that my humiliation couldn't get any worse. I had never seen Pastor's son struggle financially; he seemed to have plenty of money. He reached into his wallet, pulled out a dollar bill, and handed it to me.

It was times like these that my resentment grew and turned to bitterness. But bitterness didn't spur me to action against injustice—that wasn't how my lifetime of spiritual abuse had trained me to respond. Instead, I felt a tremendous sense of guilt, which I believed was conviction from God. A shame cycle ensued, and I prayed for forgiveness for my bitter spirit. We were on the front lines of spiritual battle at Freedom Village, and our hearts weren't in the right place if money mattered to us. God expected more from us, and animosity toward Pastor was the same as being resentful of God.

I've heard it said that a person's understanding of God is influenced by their experience with their father. However, my perception of God was linked to Pastor instead because his impact on my life was even greater than my own father's, mostly because he held more authority over me. Pastor could be your best friend and your greatest encourager. He could also rip your spirit to shreds if you crossed him. I was always trying to please him, and still I could find myself in his bull's-eye at any moment. There was no worse place to be than in that bull's-eye. So maybe there was truth to the established wisdom. I often felt this way about my own Heavenly Father.

AS I NEARED my due date, I was looking forward to being home with our baby. Like many other women on staff had done, I was planning to take an indefinite break from my job so I could be a stay-at-home mom. Those plans changed, however, during a staff meeting late in my third trimester. Pastor announced, seemingly out of nowhere, that women would not be allowed to be stay-at-home moms anymore. We needed to pull our own weight. Staying at home was backing away from the teenagers that God had called us to minister to. I was reminded of my feelings during my early days of dating Mike: Was Pastor really changing a rule every time I approached the boundary line?

The standard was clear: God first. Ministry second. Family third. It has taken me a very long time to realize the wrongness of this paradigm. However, it was effective in making sure staff members put dorm shifts and touring trips ahead of the needs of their spouse or children. My heart sank. I had no choice: I would get three months of maternity leave, and then I would be back to work at the school *and* traveling with the New Life Singers. Shockingly, this was the first time a red flag shot up in my mind at something Pastor said.

It was a hot August day when our baby started her forty-six-hour journey into the world. When we reached the hospital, the staff told me my labor wasn't progressing quickly enough and gave me medication to speed along the process, to no avail. Our baby was still safe, but my body wasn't cooperating. It was a rough labor, in which so many things that could go wrong did. Finally, Leah was born. I had a hard time breastfeeding, as Leah's poor head was bruised and tender from the long, traumatic birth. As it turns out, holding the back of your newborn's head is quite crucial to successful breastfeeding, and I couldn't do it without hurting her. My need to be good and right, to please everyone and keep a smile on my face, was proving hard to keep up. At Freedom Village, I needed to control myself in order to survive, and I did. But newborns? They are not easily controlled. My mental health was shaken within the first few days of parenthood as I realized I could not remain in control. I felt unequipped, as many new mothers do. But the spiritual atmosphere I was returning to as a mother was not kind to people who were not in control.

Mike and I spent about two days in the hospital, then headed home to our new life. I was given three months of maternity leave, and Mike went back to work immediately. I was completely unprepared. Even though I had no idea what I was doing, the first few months went by quickly and without major incident as Mike and I navigated the waters of new parenthood together. Parental leave was a blur for me, but it was a nice respite from daily life at Freedom Village. I tried not to think about my dwindling three months with Leah. The campus had a nursery and daycare, so Leah would go to daycare from eight a.m. to three p.m. every day when I went back to work. I was keeping an eye on other women who were resisting Pastor's new rule forbidding stay-at-home moms on staff—and it wasn't going well for them. Once people challenged Pastor on his rules, they either conceded that he was right or left Freedom Village. My own mind threw out accusations: I was horrible and wrong for wanting to stop touring, stop teaching, and stay home to raise my baby.

My parental leave ended just in time for the Christmas cantata touring season, where Mike and I were top of the list for testimonies to be shared. Here was the rare story of a program kid who married a staff kid, now contributing to the next generation of Freedom Village. It earned us so much favor from Pastor, which was frankly intoxicating. So we took three-month-old Leah on the road to fundraise for Freedom Village.

The ministry grew increasingly demanding the more Mike and I matured in our marriage and in our new role as parents. Pastor now required the Senior Staff deans to work the night watch shift, previously a responsibility that was given only to Junior Staff members. These work responsibilities pulled Mike away from home for more hours, and a couple of nights a week he wouldn't even be in bed with me all night. His eight-hour dorm shifts started at five a.m., eight a.m., or three p.m., plus he could have a night watch from eleven at night to five in the morning. I taught at the school from eight to three, pulled a shift in the girls dorm once a week from five to eleven p.m., and sang full-time in church and on the road. Mike had been allowed to retire from touring with New Life after Leah was born. I'm sure it was both because he would have more time to work in the boys dorm and because it would make my life harder on tour. I was twenty-two years old, still loading into a twelve-passenger van with a bunch of teenagers—now also with a car seat, a diaper bag, and an infant—for five- and six-day tours. Mike and I were both exhausted in every way possible. Our life was consumed with serving in ministry, leaving very little time for us to do anything for our family.

Not surprisingly, it didn't take long for severe anxiety to manifest, and I couldn't perform my way out of it. I was overwhelmed with irrational fears. A friend would ask to hold the baby, and I would pass Leah to them. My mind then played out a scenario where the friend threw Leah into the wall, spurring me to panic. Horrific, graphic images kept flooding my mind while I stood there, determined not to show that I was on the verge of a panic attack. I was ashamed of these intrusive thoughts, so I tried throwing up the old wall with cries of "I'm fine!" Once again, I felt like something was very wrong with me, and once again, I told no one. I wasn't sleeping. It was impossible to act normal, so I pulled away from my friends, and even Mike and I started drifting apart.

During this first year, I was convinced that everything always had to be one hundred percent "right" with Leah; if it wasn't, I would completely melt down. I worked to get Leah on a schedule so that she fed and napped at consistent times, even when we were touring. She was regularly sleeping through the night by eight months old. If one little thing altered my schedule for Leah, I would panic. If she missed a nap, it was the end of the world. If she cried when we were out shopping, I believed that everyone in the store thought I was a horrible mother who couldn't control her child, so I'd leave a full shopping cart in the aisle and get out as fast as I could. I was out of control. I was coming unglued.

I knew my behavior was affecting Mike, and I questioned if he wondered where his wife had gone. I hadn't relaxed in a solid year. I was convinced that horrible things were about to happen all the time. When we traveled as a family, I was sure we were going to collide with other cars. Suffering through chest pains and sweaty palms in total silence, I couldn't let anyone, including Mike, see what I was going through—and as tiring as it was to feel emotions like that, it was even more exhausting to hide them.

As I sank further into postpartum anxiety and depression, Freedom Village kept demanding more from us. Mike's retirement from New Life was extremely hard on me. I saw my husband even less as I took Leah on the road by myself, even though I had long since lost my ambition to sing and travel. Packing in for long van rides, setting up and performing at one venue, tearing down, going to another venue to do it all again, then sleeping in a hotel alone with my baby...I didn't want to do it anymore. Even worse, I felt guilty for that.

In my panic and shame, I was once again convinced I needed to fix myself before coming to God for help. I was running myself ragged in the name of ministry while spiritually empty and full of fear. I was afraid I would be the next staff person to be ripped into emotionally. I was afraid to ask to leave New Life. I was afraid of the strain on my marriage because Mike and I never had time to properly communicate. I was afraid of ruining Leah. And on a much deeper level than I realized then, I was afraid that this was going to be the rest of my life.

Nothing rocks a person's world more than having a child. I was beginning to comprehend the constant burden borne by parents on staff at Freedom Village. Pastor, disguised as our spiritual authority, used the message of serving God full-time as a means to control and break families. I couldn't name it at the time, but I had a growing dread about raising a family in that environment. Something had to give.

Although I had entertained the idea as a teenager of leaving Freedom Village to move to Mississippi for another full-time ministry, I had never thought about leaving without Pastor's approval. That, in my mind, equated to leaving God's will. The idea of escaping Freedom Village to lead a normal life was a forbidden thought. The first time it crossed my mind, I was doing something incredibly mundane: peeing. I vividly remember sitting on the toilet in our house, and I thought about what life would look like twenty years down the road. A heavy weight sank onto my heart as I imagined Leah as a teenager at Freedom Village.

My first reaction was that this illicit thought was morally wrong. I was trained to counsel people about the dangers of being out of God's will if they thought about leaving Freedom Village. Even though I had visited so much of the real world with the New Life Singers and Ballet Magnificat, I saw it as dark, scary, and bad. Since I was a small child, I had traveled with the eyes of a missionary: The outside world was a sinful, depraved mission field, and I had been commissioned by Jesus to save it. That world was to be avoided at all costs, unless it was for evangelism. I could hardly bear the thought of leaving Freedom Village without Pastor's approval and the resultant risk of being out from under God's hand.

But even as I felt fear (that I now know was not of God), I also experienced a strange sense of peace. It was as if God met me in that bathroom and assured me that wherever we ended up, He would not leave us. "You can leave. You can go *anywhere*, and I am with you always. You can never be separated from love, no matter where you go or what you do, even outside the walls of Freedom Village," whispered a very still, very small inner voice.

The words were so clearly God's, though so obviously not like the God I had known until then. It was the first ray of hope I remember that suggested I could still follow the one true God outside the bounds of Freedom Village. I was still in darkness—that's true—but it felt like it was almost time for a sunrise.

11

THE LEAVING

WHY WAS I at Freedom Village anyway? I've heard countless staff people, including my parents, say, "We stayed for the teenagers." It's possible that all the first-generation staff were, in fact, called by God to be a part of those troubled teenagers' lives at Freedom Village. I wasn't there for them. I had decided to stay when I was seventeen because I knew I wanted to follow the path of singing instead of dancing. Unlike others on staff, I don't believe I ever had a calling to work at Freedom Village. Instead, I was like the many program kids who finished their required year at Freedom Village and chose to remain as staff. Frankly, I stayed because I was afraid of what would happen if I left. I had no noble reason for working there, no sense of God-given purpose keeping me there...only fear.

That doesn't mean staying at Freedom Village was a mistake: I didn't know what I didn't know. Certainly I didn't have an outside perspective to counteract what I had been raised with. And my family and I found good and did good there. My parents helped teens through the program and clung to Christ and each other, despite Pastor's twisted teachings and misshapen doctrines. My siblings and I each met our spouses at Freedom Village. We sang, traveled, and served.

Even though I was burned out and always anxious, I still found meaning as I toured with the New Life Singers, particularly when I had the opportunity to share my testimony. God used my personal story of pain to reach others who were struggling, and I'll never regret the impact that had. But once I had my own children, my life's purpose rightfully shifted. Perhaps my parents should have put our family first, and maybe I should have decided to prioritize my own young family over the ministry sooner, but God is a master at reshaping even our stories of trauma. He blends an ugly stain into new, vibrant colors within our lives. Those who know His love will see it and cling to Him, even when nothing else makes sense.

I CAME HOME one spring day in 2011 to find Mike ironing a collared shirt, which was strange because he rarely dressed up for work. He also had an unusual look of panic on his face. He was preparing to go to Pastor's office to beg to keep his job—both of our jobs, in fact. I was pregnant with our second child and Mike had just gotten fired.

One of Mike's responsibilities as boys' dean was to handle any money the program kids received from home or from supporters. (Sometimes money from donors and parents actually did go to the teenagers who needed it.) The program teens draw from these accounts to spend on campus or if they go off-property for a special occasion. Mike had taken a program boy out one day and brought home an envelope of change and receipts that needed to be deposited back into the boy's account the next day. But Mike forgot, leaving the envelope at home as he left for work that morning. When Mike was on dorm duty that night, the boy asked whether Mike had deposited the money back into his account.

"No," Mike joked, "my wife and I spent it on groceries."

The ensuing chain of events should come as no surprise at Freedom Village. The boy went to the head dean. Instead of talking to Mike, the head dean went to the program director. Instead of talking to Mike, the program director went to the school principal. Instead of talking to Mike, the head dean, the program director, and the school principal together went to Pastor directly to report that Mike was stealing money from kids' accounts. Instead of talking to Mike, Pastor simply fired us.

Mike, who works hard and does right by others, was going to have to fight an uphill battle to save our livelihoods and our lives as we knew them. I felt the sting of betrayal from those fellow staff people, who we considered friends. Lest you think I was any better than them, though, know that I had thrown my fair share of people under the bus in this ministry. As a teacher, I once worked hard to help a program girl who had always struggled academically to reach the end of our high school program. She was already at the Junior Staff level, progressing on her last workbook before being able to graduate, when I discovered her cheating. This girl was on the verge of getting into trouble for other things, and I knew it. I also knew I would be rewarded for adding to the drama. How many times had I seen the same scenario play out? Once someone was on Pastor's bad list, the staff was in a feeding frenzy to come up with dirt on them, continuing the toxic targeting cycle and earning themselves a spot on Pastor's good list.

I reported her cheating to the school principal. The girl was demoted from Junior Staff all the way down to No Level, a position I knew all too well. I was oddly satisfied, knowing that I had delivered the clincher in her downfall. Perhaps I could justify my disclosure as in a different category from gossip about Mike's supposed "stealing." After all, I had seen the cheating with my own eyes. Honestly, I felt horrible too. Was that because I knew I had done something wrong? Did I know that I could have or should have handled her situation differently and brought about better results? Or was my regret merely because I was afraid the student would be angry with me? The next day, it could be me getting thrown under the bus. I had used my authority to remain in Pastor's good graces. No one really had anyone else's back at Freedom Village, as I had seen time and time again.

Since no one in the ministry had his back, Mike went into his meeting with Pastor alone, wearing his crisply ironed shirt. He came out with our lives still intact. Mike and I were allowed to stay at Freedom Village, but Mike was demoted from boys' dean to the maintenance department. It was a gloriously low-profile position, and he actually had the best time working there. My spirit was breaking, though. I felt like I was drowning. I was battling horrible anxiety, I was overworked, and I was feeling more bitter by the day.

AS THE SCHOOL year drew to a close, the staff began to notice that Pastor's wife was missing. Throughout his fundamentalist teachings, Pastor had made it clear that he abhorred women who "wore the pants" in a relationship—an irony I can't ignore, because this was the wife who had bent the rules so women could literally wear pants at Freedom Village. I was convinced that God didn't like strong women. If Pastor's wife was strong-willed enough to leave him, God must not love Pastor's wife. While other staff people started to question where she was, I just assumed we were all better off without her.

At the next staff meeting, to "clear up confusion," Pastor shared a bizarre story about his missing wife. She left him, he said. He suspected she was a lesbian, and he had hired private investigators to follow her so he could prove it. She was apparently also into the occult. Obviously, we were all forbidden to get in touch with her. He was setting up his reasons for divorce—considered a sin by many fundamentalist Christians—and airing his wife's supposed dirty laundry, all during a staff meeting. It was awkward and blatantly inappropriate. What Pastor said was so out of place and unbelievable that many staff began to discern that something was not right. It seemed Pastor had begun hammering the nail into his own coffin.

Soon, a new woman appeared on campus who "felt called to work at Freedom Village." Before long, it was obvious that she and Pastor were dating and in love—while he was still married. I'm not confused about the historical timeline here and accidentally repeating a story. Freedom Village had in fact already weathered this storm fifteen years earlier, when Pastor's previous wife left him and his new girlfriend came on the scene before he was even divorced.

This time Pastor's new girlfriend was at least half his age, also divorced, and had two young children. Everyone in the ministry was simply expected to accept her into the fold as his new woman. Such relationships were practices that clearly went against Pastor's teachings, yet history was repeating itself.

I really believe Pastor thought he would get away with it again. But something about this situation struck the staff as absurd, and common sense began to prevail in many of our brainwashed minds. Pastor was *wrong*, and it was becoming obvious to those around him. More people were questioning him at once than ever before.

With Pastor's reputation in tatters among his staff (and likely the program kids as well), the board of Freedom Village, my father included, finally confronted Pastor and asked him to step down as the head of the ministry. Pastor was risking catastrophic loss for the ministry by refusing to be held accountable for his actions. If there was any hope of saving Freedom Village, he would need to retire and let someone else take the lead. If Pastor refused to step down, they warned, most of his staff would leave.

"Let them," Pastor responded.

That might have been the first moment the truth was revealed that Pastor didn't care about anyone other than himself. It seemed clear that if he truly cared about troubled teenagers and the vision of Freedom Village, he would step down to let someone else run the ministry. Instead, he showed that he cared the most about being the leader of Freedom Village, and *that* was what he wanted to protect.

While Pastor's drama was unfolding, I was in my own little world—working, touring, and raising an almost-two-year-old as my August due date approached. I was operating in the fog of burnout and pregnancy brain.

As the author of this book, I'd like to tell you that *the leaving* of Freedom Village is crystal clear in my mind. When I say *the leaving*, I mean the half a year or so that brought a slow understanding of the mere existence of the possibility that Mike and I could leave on our own. It was a whole process of watching Pastor's behavior, feeling confused, hearing more staff than I'd ever heard at once talk among themselves about Pastor's wrongness, watching other staff resign, and finally feeling it sink into my mind that life as I had known it was going to change.

In the last three months of this process, I spent most of my time at home. I was riding out my last days as a mom of one while listening to the increasingly unbelievable news in the ministry. I remember hearing that a consistent line of staff people outside

Pastor's office waited their turn to go in and hand him their resignations.

With every staff friend who resigned, I felt little shifts within me until I finally thought, "What if *we* left? We could leave." In the context of so many people I respected choosing to resign from the ministry, the thought wasn't as scary as it might have been. Board members said that God *told them* to resign and that they felt the peace of God about it. These things apparently gave me permission to consider that forbidden thought, and once I did, I found the idea exciting and intriguing. At age twenty-four, these new thoughts about leaving didn't include the desire to please Pastor. Rather, I started to feel something else that was new to me: hope.

One of the most fascinating things about God's kingdom, as I know it now, is that death comes *before* life. You must come to the end of yourself before you can step into a new life and be reborn. We are born into sin, and sin brings forth death. But in the reality of Christ, death is not the end. We face the judgment of our souls and discover the good news that we have been forgiven. This revelation of grace saves us. It propels us forward, out of the clutches of death and into new life. Death is defeated by God's love. This is salvation, as I know it now.

For me and Mike to get to our new life, the life we knew had to die. We would have to walk away from the life that we had been brainwashed to believe was God's will. Before those little shifts added up to a massive change in direction, I never would have guessed that leaving would actually set me free.

12

OUT FROM THE INSIDE

IN A STROKE of what I can only think of as divine timing, Mike tentatively raised the question of leaving with me only days after I first had the forbidden thought. Seeing Pastor behave so far outside the bounds of morality had shaken his mind open too.

"What if?" we wondered.

What if we left?

Where would we go?

What work could he get?

What would happen to my family?

Mike later told me that he hadn't known what to expect when he brought up the idea of us leaving. I could have felt terrified once the opportunity to leave Freedom Village became real. Maybe I should have been terrified. This was the only place I had ever lived. Yet all I felt was hope.

I thought about silly things, like how nice it would be to wear clothes I wanted to wear. To listen to music I actually liked. To sleep in on a Sunday with Mike and skip church if we wanted to. I would be allowed to have a Facebook account. Maybe I would even wear a tight shirt or see what wine tasted like. I would be free to choose. The possibility of *that* was enough to begin driving the fear out of me.

We knew we couldn't make a huge life decision like this unless we felt God leading us to it. For the first time in my life, I sought direction from God alone, with no attachment to Pastor and no consideration of what he would think. I experienced sovereignty over my own mind, and it felt good. Pastor didn't have the final say, though it took years to retrain my brain to consciously seek my own thoughts, instead of defaulting to Pastor's spiritual thinking. Every time I opened my Bible or sought God in prayer, I knew it was time to go. Even beyond sensing peace about leaving, I was excited! Staff families were resigning daily; it was like the biblical story of the Israelite slaves being led out of Egypt. Watching people I trusted leave—and seeing that they weren't being struck down by lightning (or God)—helped convince me that *maybe* Pastor had been wrong about the outside. I certainly didn't want to stay if my family left (an option we had all discussed together), though they hadn't yet. Amid all these considerations, I went into labor.

Mike and I welcomed our son, Noah, into our very uncertain and unstable world at the end of August 2011. In the hospital, my second baby in my arms, I was confident that God was going to work everything out for our good, no matter what our family chose to do. Once I believed that, I knew I wanted to leave.

The day after the birth of their grandson, my parents resigned from Freedom Village. My sister and her husband did as well.

That decided it: Mike, Leah, Noah, and I would go too.

We were *all* leaving.

WHEN NOAH WAS RELEASED from the hospital, Mike and I returned with our baby to the house we knew wasn't our home anymore. Mike resigned on our behalf days after Noah's birth. We were homeless. We were jobless. Together, we had severed the cords that connected me to Freedom Village.

I never said goodbye to Pastor.

After resigning, we were given a month to find somewhere else to live. Leah was two years old and completely oblivious to what was happening. Noah was a colicky newborn who cried all day and night. Mike and I felt joyful about our decision, but life was happening fast. We were relying on God not only to point us in the right direction but to carry us as well. We were far from the only staff who resigned without a backup plan. New jobs and homes weren't waiting on the outside for any of us. In the house we would soon have to vacate, I had a teetering toddler, a constantly wailing newborn, and a husband pacing like a caged lion, trying to find some kind of job that could help us get on our feet. In the midst of this storm, I was perfectly calm. Given my mental health history, it would make more sense if I were a mess. Instead, these were some of the times I recall feeling the comforting presence of God more than ever before. Moments of panic did strike, but they were quickly replaced by a sense of peace washing over me. I knew we would be okay.

Pieces started to fall into place. My parents were able to continue living in their house after leaving Freedom Village, and the house across the street from theirs had been vacant for years. My dad asked around to see who owned it: Would the owners consider renting it out to our little family? One day later, Mike and I had a home to live in. To me, this was a dream: a big country house with three bedrooms and plenty of land for six hundred dollars a month. It cost less than some one-bedroom apartments we were looking at elsewhere. Because of both Noah and Leah, it was also a comfort to know my parents would be across the street. Nearby, a shed- and cabin-building business was hiring, and Mike got a job as an entry-level carpenter.

The first morning in our new house, I opened my eyes to bright streaks of sunshine pouring in through the windows. The air felt cleaner and fresher, even as I watched tiny dust particles dance in the early morning sunbeams against the sheer white curtains we had pulled out of a box the day before to make the room feel lived in. I looked around and took in this beautiful new house. Leah was upstairs in her new bedroom, with newborn Noah across the hall in his new nursery. So much had changed in such a short time.

We had done what I had watched so many others do: We left Freedom Village. Our departure was likely easier than those of staff families in the past because so many other people left around the same time. When all was said and done, Freedom Village lost more than two-thirds of its staff. My dad was among those who fought for the ministry before he finally decided to leave. In spite of everything, my dad loved Pastor and tried until the end to help him recognize his own sin, just as he had done more than a decade earlier when he found Pastor and his girlfriend alone together. But Pastor was going to run his ministry on his terms, no matter the losses—even losses as great as my father. It was ultimately Pastor's stubbornness that paved my family's path from inside Freedom Village to actual freedom outside.

My father gave me advice years before that I've never forgotten, even though I couldn't accept it at the time. He told me that God's will isn't a place. It isn't a job or a relationship with a partner or spouse. It isn't a decision you make at a fork in the road. It's not a protection that God gives you, or that He yanks back if you haven't lived right enough for Him. *God's will is a state of being.* His will, quite simply, is that we know Him. It's why we were made in the first place. We have all been given a desire that can only be satisfied by knowing the heart of God. My dad tried to teach me this truth, and I believed him—to a point. But with Pastor as my spiritual authority, I received two conflicting truths: that God's will was simply for me to know Him, and that God's will was for me to obey Pastor. For the longest time, I believed the latter.

I had grown up assuming that if I were ever to leave Freedom Village, I would be terrified. I had heard the staff who had left and then returned recall how they felt God abandoned them once they had left His will. But once I made that choice, I never felt like leaving Freedom Village was the wrong decision, and I didn't want to return. I was lucky, though, to have support and a foundation in place that many program kids and staff didn't.

My parents taught me that God was with me all the time. It was as if they had planted a seed way down deep in my soul, deep enough that it remained unseen for a long time. Pastor poisoned that belief and stunted my spiritual growth by planting lies about God's nature in the soil of my mind. When I believed that God was like Pastor, my parents' truth was twisted: Who wants to be ever-connected to a monster? But that kernel of truth was still with me as I left Freedom Village alongside my family and felt God's peace.

Ex-Villagers who have reached out to me on *Out from the Inside* have shared that Pastor's picture of God laid a foundation at the very beginning of their Christian faith. They felt abandoned by God when they left Freedom Village. They talked about how in that impression of absence, they assumed God had removed Himself and His blessing from their lives because they turned away from our ministry. Some people fell back into old, harmful habits, their lives fell apart, and often they went back to Freedom Village. Sometimes they would thrive again after they returned.

Freedom Village was a center for rehabilitation that did not prepare its teens or young adults for a life and faith in the real world. The program brought in teens, introduced them to God, and pressured them to accept Christ as their Savior. The teens were then loaded down with responsibilities as they lived this new Christian life away from their homes. Freedom Village put them on the road to advertise for the ministry through their testimonies. Postcards featuring their faces were mailed out to supporters, who sent money that kept the ministry doors open. The teenagers listened to sermons about how the outside world was getting worse. They were promoted and rewarded until they reached the end of their one-year commitment, and then it was time to stay or leave. They were told they belonged there; this was their family now. They could spend the rest of their lives at Freedom Village, helping other teens who were just like them. If they wanted to leave, they were given the other option—to serve fries at McDonald's—and who would choose that over serving God full-time?

Let's say the teen decided to leave. They were pulled into several meetings with staff members like me who tried to convince them to stay at Freedom Village. Once it was clear that the teen intended to leave, they were sent away, with every person who had spent a year or more pouring into them now telling them they were making a huge mistake. Communication was severed. No one helped them find housing. Their relationship with God was still new (and its foundation was flawed), yet no one set them up with a church or community group that would help them make it outside the program or the ministry. Cut off from all support, their new spiritual intellect told them that maybe God was mad at them. They were on their own, and they were not prepared for success in the real world.

My challenges on the outside were not exactly like those of the program kids who left. Mine were tempered by the faith my parents taught me and the support of my family, but I still carried Freedom Village with me. Despite being out of the environment where I was immersed in insecurity and fear of consequences, I found that anxiety and depression began to work themselves back into my life. Pastor was gone, though his thousands of sermons and messages remained in my mind. I remained a victim of the accusing voice of condemnation. At some moments, I wondered whether Pastor had been right and punishment was waiting around the corner for us because we weren't in full-time Christian service.

There were staff people who stayed at Freedom Village and who dared to talk to us on the outside. They said Pastor was preaching nearly every sermon about those of us who left. He told the remaining staff and program kids that we were having Satanic rituals at my parents' house to pray curses over the ministry. He predicted that he would stand over our children's graves one day as a consequence for our leaving the will of God. I knew with certainty that the utter peace and love I felt when we left Freedom Village was from God. Still, condemnation didn't stop eating away at me. I had crawled out of one Hell only to realize that the demons who had haunted me at Freedom Village were going to follow me wherever I went.

13

AFTERSHOCKS

"I JUST WANTED to move on with my life and pretend Freedom Village never happened," ex-Villagers tell me. "But it followed me, and I thought I was crazy." In the following handful of years, I became more certain that I was crazy, too: I couldn't tell what was real and what was not, spiritually speaking.

The first winter after we left Freedom Village, my life took a hard, sharp turn into what I call the blurry years. As we settled into the realities of life, my sense of peace faded, the same peace that had given me assurance we were on the right path. Instead, I was spiritually reeling from stepping outside of my lifelong bubble and into a totally incomprehensible new life. Postpartum anxiety reared its head again, and now I had two very small children who needed me every moment of the day. I began having mild panic attacks in the car, sure every minute of a long drive with Mike at the wheel that we were going to get into an accident. Fear tainted everything I did. Even my sleep wasn't safe. I had horrible dreams where I would hurt my children. I would wake up from the nightmares shaking and petrified.

Our lovely new home, so recently bright, airy, and fresh-feeling, now felt oppressive and messy. I was often depressed. Dirty dishes sat in the sink for days on end, and mountains of laundry grew in every corner as I struggled simply to get through the day. Mike was steadfast, working hard in his physically demanding position as a carpenter. The situation at home seemed to frustrate him, though, which fueled my insecurity, making me believe he hated me. We had trouble communicating, which was not surprising given our history at Freedom Village.

I was always on the verge of breaking down and obsessive about feeding, play, and nap schedules for the kids. If they cried instead of sleeping, rage would well up in me like I had never felt before—not at them per se but at being in a situation I couldn't control. I had survived Freedom Village by controlling as much as I could. If my babies missed their nap, my brain told me, their schedule would be shot, the day would be ruined, and I'd be stuck home alone with a whiny, overtired two-year-old and a cranky, teething four-month-old. I lashed out at the kids, and I lashed out at Mike. What I couldn't understand at the time was that my anxiety ran deeper than my present circumstances. I wasn't just tired from late-night breastfeeding and early-morning diaper changes. My soul was exhausted from trying to hold myself together. I didn't have Pastor to constantly please all the time anymore, but I had enough years of confusing his voice with God's to keep me in an eternal loop of spiritual confusion. I felt inept and unable to remain in control of my life. The accusing voice in my head never stopped telling me that I was only one sin away from earning God's terrible consequences. The punishment for the anger I was feeling might be my kid getting cancer or Mike dropping dead at work. All because of my sin.

I should have reached out to my mom for help through my exhaustion and stress, but I didn't know how to ask for it. I didn't even realize I needed help. Whenever I became overwhelmed or depressed, I was so ashamed at my own imperfection that I spiraled downward. I was trying to locate the sin that was causing my feelings rather than looking to the very beliefs I held about God and myself as the possible culprits of my debilitating anxiety.

On Christmas Eve, I went to Walmart by myself, which was a rare and wonderful gift for a young mom of two. Noah was four months old, and I had finally been able to start exercising again. I'd stopped breastfeeding, and I was in the process of switching to a new birth control. As I pushed my cart down one aisle after another, blissfully encumbered by groceries but not babies, a wave of nausea hit. Immediately after, so did the realization that my period was late that month. *"No way,"* my mind screamed. I beelined to the personal care aisle and bought a pregnancy test. Overflowing with anxiety, I went into the Walmart bathroom to take the test. I was going to be a mom of three much sooner than I had planned.

I cried so hard as I drove home that I couldn't see the road in front of me. Though I felt horrible for not appreciating the gift of a pregnancy, I also didn't feel ready in any way for another baby. I don't remember much about that Christmas, or about my pregnancy with our third child, for that matter. This truly was the first of my blurry years.

By the time our feisty little Claire came into the picture, I had come to accept the idea of another baby joining the roost so soon. We decided that Claire would be our last baby. Mike and I now had three August babies: a three-year-old, a one-year-old, and a newborn. I was twenty-five and he was twenty-nine. We had our work cut out for us.

Mike had been at his job for a year when Claire was born. My mom and I had partnered to reopen her old ballet school, this time as a performing arts school that also offered classes in piano, voice, modern dance, and musical theater. I was thrilled to be dancing again, and I adored teaching ballet. I loved choreographing and enjoyed the process of bringing my creative visions to life. In the studio I would find moments of joy and peace, but fear inevitably chased them away. Apparently, I was still not free from my past. In the Freedom Village mindset, every well-worn neuronal pathway led to condemnation. If I was happy, I felt condemned because I wasn't suffering for Christ. If I was depressed, I felt condemned because I was supposed to be a joyful ambassador for Christ. Unseen and unrecognized, that old cycle of "obedience brings blessings; disobedience brings consequences" plagued my thought processes.

I was in the trenches, maybe as much as any soldier for the Lord ever was. I had a toddler, a baby, and a newborn. I still didn't know what the heck I was doing. My need for control died a slow and painful death as I learned that I couldn't possibly have things the way I wanted them all the time. These kids ran my every waking moment. And this wasn't always a bad thing! My kids are awesome, with magnificent senses of humor and imaginations. Those days were some of the sweetest times I'll ever know. I nursed Claire while I watched Noah learn to walk and Leah become her own little person. We had picnics in the yard and played with our neighbor's free-ranging chickens. I pulled all three kids in the wagon to take long walks along our quiet country road. I soaked up these moments as much as I could because I knew there would be no more new babies to repeat them with. I was relieved to find that, even though I hadn't been a babysitter or a baby whisperer, I loved my kids unconditionally.

My children were not the only ones growing and changing. As I also grew up and began to learn about myself, those years brought me to some seriously low places. The three little people I spent my days with didn't care about my self-perception, but it struck me that I had no idea who I was. The mental health problems I had as a teenager grew, mutated, and became a nightmare as I navigated the wide world outside of Freedom Village. It might come as no surprise, but I fought old demons of self-esteem and body dysmorphia as my body changed over the course of three pregnancies in rapid succession. And just as I had when I was a teen, I thought if I ignored them and kept them hidden, they would go away. It seems some lessons must be learned more than once.

I was wrong when I thought I had escaped Pastor's control because I left Freedom Village. I should have foreseen how hard it would be to get him out of my head. We are a rare breed, those of us who have been through Freedom Village. More souls than you can imagine are wading through that wreckage of leaving, feeling like God has disappeared. Thousands are out here in the real world waiting for God to withdraw His blessings and condemn them at any moment, constantly striving to please Him and live up to a standard that no one can attain. Being raised in Freedom Village was a unique experience, but I cannot unsee the spiritual abuse that also exists in church culture today. People are opening their eyes to abusive teachings and practices in churches they have dearly loved and devoted their hearts and time to, and they are leaving. They are reeling with spiritual confusion because the people they had entrusted with spiritual authority were using the name of God to manipulate and control them for personal gain. I used to think my story would only be relevant to those who experienced Freedom Village. I wrote for myself, and for them. Now, I am writing for all of us: Freedom Village insiders and real-world outsiders. We've suffered the same spiritual pain.

14

EPIPHANY

THOUGH MANY OF the early years after I left Freedom Village passed in a blur, one date stands out absolutely stark in my memory. On the evening of December 7, 2018, the deconstruction of my worldview began. Mike and I had gone to his work Christmas party and decided to extend the night with friends, heading out to a bar for a drink and some late-night salty snacks. I had recently finished blogging about my experience at Freedom Village, and I was beginning to question whether I had been wrong about who God is. While watching a game of pool, I struck up a conversation with one of Mike's coworkers, whose name was Patrick. He was a Christian, and at ten p.m. in a small-town bar, he started telling me about his recent spiritual awakening and resulting freedom from fear.

"I have so much fear in my life, I'm afraid to even think about it," I confessed self-consciously when he finished his story.

Truthfully, I was unsettled by this guy. Even though I had left Freedom Village seven years earlier, my heart was still apprehensive about being seen in a worldly place like a bar. I assumed that most Christians who drank or went to bars suspected it might be wrong but did it anyway. Yet here was a man who moved through this worldly place with such genuine peace, seeking out deep conversations. He didn't seem concerned about his reputation while he sipped his alcohol and shared with me how beautiful and loving he knew God to be. Normally, I would have classified this type of Christian as lukewarm. Churchgoers are warned about the lukewarms: a scary breed of people who live however they want and still think they can love God; the cherry-pickers who take Bible verses out of context so they can justify their sin. I was taught to fear ever becoming one of *those* Christians, because God will essentially spit them out of His mouth.

Despite that, something about Patrick's words to me pierced through the darkness and fear. He shed tears as he shared lyrics from Audrey Assad's song "Evergreen" that helped him on his journey. He told me healing from trauma and fear is possible. I have no doubt that Jesus met me at the bar that night; He spoke through a regular man so filled with wonder at his own encounter with God that he couldn't help but tell others. It was so authentic, and I was envious that he was so free. And it wasn't a lawless freedom. It was the real thing.

In the following days, I couldn't stop thinking about the lyrics of "Evergreen," which asserted that there is something beyond fear that we could feel. But doesn't God want us to be afraid? Doesn't the Bible say that the fear of the Lord is the beginning of wisdom? Isn't it a healthy thing to be afraid of sinning? Sin has consequences. Shouldn't we fear sin? Everything in my religious arsenal *screamed* at me to run away from the idea that my fear was doing anything other than protecting me. I did the only thing I could think to do: I found Patrick on Facebook, sent a friend request, and followed up with a message.

I told him I was intrigued by his lack of fear and obvious intimacy with God—but I had some questions:

Wasn't he afraid of being seen at a bar, partaking in alcohol, in the midst of unbelievers?

Did he ever question whether he was sinning?

Did he even care that he might *be* sinning?

How could he be so peaceful and filled with childlike wonder?

How could he sleep at night?!

I mentioned how afraid I was to make mistakes, how I spent so many sleepless nights paralyzed by the consequences and punishments from God I might be heaping on my life because of known, or unknown, sin.

"My fear is that if something is, indeed, a sin and I do it anyway...that's a scary thought," I wrote.

I read over my message, decided I sounded off the wall, then hit send before I could talk myself out of it. I felt like I was doing something wrong. Was it inappropriate to send a private Facebook message to a man other than my husband? Maybe the fact that I was even thinking of that was reason enough to write another message and apologize.

"Avoid all appearances of evil!" screamed a voice in my mind. "If it even looks questionable, you should avoid it."

And yet, I had sent the message. I felt so stupid as I played out one imagined scenario after the next. My anxiety told me that he would reply, "Hey, you're extremely inappropriate. Don't message me privately again, creeper." I wished I were a skilled computer hacker so I could delete the message before he ever saw it.

His reply notification popped up nearly seven hours later. He didn't shut me down or shame me. Much like Jesus would do, he answered my questions with a question of his own: "I'm interested to hear more about what you meant by 'My fear is that if something is, indeed, a sin and I do it anyway...that's a scary thought.' Scary in what way, exactly?"

This was a life-altering moment for me. Patrick was essentially asking me, a sister in Christ, what exactly I was afraid of. What *was* I afraid of? When I really thought about it, I had no idea. I only knew that I was very afraid. For the first time in my life, I allowed myself to follow that fear. I dug into it deeper. What was I afraid of, really?

Punishment.

Retribution.

Getting what I deserved.

Disappointing the God I loved.

Disappointing people.

Being punished for anything wrong someone might find out about me. Pastor had taught me to feel that way in relation to him...but also to feel that way about God.

Since birth, that type of fear was all I ever knew. What I couldn't see clearly at the time was that my whole mind had been hijacked by a lifetime of trauma in a spiritually abusive environment, an environment in which I had no control over whether I'd be rewarded or punished on any given day.

I'm far from the first person to have been spiritually manipulated, and Pastor's narcissism, insecurity, quick temper, and need for control are not unique in the world. Imagine a successful politician or corporate businessman. Add some dark, warped views of God formed through years of the person's own trauma rather than intimacy with God. This charismatic man concludes that God is primarily an angry, wrathful being who only wants to use humans and who hates anyone who sins, even believers. Now give this person a pulpit to preach from and full, unquestioned authority over an entire community of people. The stage is set: Let the pain and disorder begin.

When I came onto the stage, I was harmed more deeply than others because I was raised under him from birth. At least, that's what I have come to believe. This was my "normal." The God that Pastor preached about was my foundation of faith, and, not coincidentally, that God sounded a lot like Pastor.

Spreading the gospel is central to Christianity so that "Heaven can invade Earth." Christians pray "let Thy kingdom come" in hopes that the way God's kingdom is set up in Heaven will be made manifest here on Earth. I understand this concept far more deeply today, as a state of inner *rest*. But back then, when I imagined a kingdom of people who lived according to the law of God... it looked just like Freedom Village. Everyone would be earning God's favor by "living right," and there was *one right way*. Everyone would look the same, act the same, worship the same, and recite the same creed. And worst of all, there were so many people on the outside of this kingdom. My goal was to stay inside, by any means necessary, even if it meant I was divided from most of God's people. The kingdom of God was for the elite, the ones who really wanted to be there and were prepared to serve God to work for it. My perception of the kingdom of God was a hellish, abusive environment. And the way I felt about God was how I'd always felt about Pastor. I wanted His approval more than anything. I feared the punishment He doled out for making mistakes. I wanted to do everything right by Him. Nothing felt better than knowing He was happy with me. I wanted to be used by Him. I wanted to feel like He was choosing me to be someone special. I wanted to prove I was worthy of His attention and favor.

Am I talking about God or Pastor right now? Your guess is as good as mine.

That December night, in a bar with Mike's coworker, I had gotten a glimpse of a different kind of kingdom. The man I had talked to knew God's love and was completely at rest, with nothing to prove. I had been on the outside of Freedom Village for seven years, living without the voice of Pastor teaching me about God—but somehow, my concept of God had remained unchanged.

The central question of that Facebook message was now playing constantly in my mind. *What am I so afraid of?* And I was met with the biggest blessing in my life: doubt.

What if I were wrong about God?

In this season of my life, I was exhausted and depressed. I found myself wishing I were an inanimate object; if only I could be a bowl, a rock, or even an animal, I wouldn't have to spend every waking moment ashamed of myself and dreading my inevitable mistakes. But the more I asked myself this question, the more I began to hope I *was* wrong about Him.

What if God isn't angry?

What if He isn't transactional?

What if my actions have no effect on His love for me?

To go down this path and follow this line of questioning, I would have to doubt my reality, and that was quite scary. But I suddenly wanted nothing to do with a God that looked and acted like Pastor, who I was just now seeing clearly. I wanted nothing to do with a religion that fed on fear. I wanted to tear it all down, even if that left me at spiritual ground zero.

Doubt is a slippery slope, I was always taught. If you let yourself doubt the small things, you will inevitably doubt the big things, and you might wind up with no faith at all. That was a horrifying prospect. I spent weeks debating whether to take a ride down that slippery slope. The more I considered doubting the character of God, the more I seemed to find verses, quotes, and even whole sermons that affirmed the beliefs I'd been raised with. I read Scripture about the wrath of God and the fate of those who practice sin. A growing sense of panic plagued my every waking moment—literally all day long. I fell into a rabbit hole on YouTube, watching sermons screamed by red-faced pastors who smacked their Bibles on the pulpit and called sinners to the altar, commanding them to repent or be destroyed. In the following days I was scared straight.

My fear was good, I insisted to myself. It kept me safe from doubt. Doubt leads to sin, and sin requires punishment. Keep reading the Bible. Keep going to church. Keep abstaining, keep confessing, keep trying. Even kids need a healthy dose of fear of what their parents will do if they disobey, right? My fear was healthy and necessary. And yet, that tiny voice remained.

"Maybe you're wrong," it whispered. "Maybe God is so much more than what you believe. Maybe He is nothing like Pastor."

Maybe. My heart was seeking like it never had before. Good news was finding me in the most interesting places (like at a pool table), suggesting that I might be wrong about God. Fear and hope pulled me in opposite directions. I was going to lose my mind if the tug-of-war didn't come to a permanent end. I had to face each opponent independently and decide which end of the rope to release.

My whole belief system was like a batch of soup that had been poisoned. To get rid of the poison, I had to be willing to empty the whole pot. Fear screamed that this was heresy. Hope whispered something else, something that felt like home. Words I had read in the Gospel of Matthew a thousand times before finally made perfect sense: "Whoever wants to be my disciple must deny themselves and take up their cross and follow me. For whoever wants to save their life will lose it, but whoever loses their life for me will find it."

What if that *didn't* mean "I should want to suffer" or "I must hate myself in order to love God"? What if, instead, it meant that in order to know the truth and be set free, I needed to be willing to be wrong about it all? Life had brought me to a point of complete exhaustion; needing to be right is such a heavy burden. If Christ's invitation was to come and rest, I was ready to release everything I thought I knew.

I distinctly remember lying in my bed the night I consciously decided to doubt it all. I needed to dump out the soup pot. It was the beginning of the process of deconstruction, a critical evaluation of faith that strips beliefs down to nothing.

I started by putting to death everything I had ever been taught to be true about God—even His very existence. I was led by a willingness to be wrong, something altogether new to me. That willingness took me to some places I never imagined I'd go. What if God doesn't exist? What if there is no God? We are out here on our own, flying through space without a creator or a master plan, just trying to survive and make sense of this life. Could this be true? Oddly enough, I had never considered this question in my thirty years of life. Is it a choice to believe if it has been the only option on the table? In response to *that* question, I deconstructed my faith to absolutely nothing. It was terrifying. I was like a fish attempting to breathe in the desert. I was a born-and-raised church kid contemplating whether religion itself is a manmade system designed to control the masses.

I spoke with friends who were atheists, and I listened to their experiences and perspectives. I read articles presenting compelling evidence that people have simply made up every story we have about Jesus and God. I carefully considered how I might feel if the truth was that there is no God. If I knew the truth was that we live in a world without God, could I believe it? Would I even want to believe it? There, at the hungriest place in my spiritual life, I answered yes. I wanted to know *truth*.

As someone who had held to faith my entire life like a

drowning person clings to a life preserver, being without it was wild. I wholeheartedly entertained unbelief, a side of faith I had never before been on. Some may call it heresy or madness or an exercise in nihilism, but this level of deconstruction was necessary for me (although it isn't a space I want or need to revisit).

In this process of deconstruction, of allowing this spiritual storm I couldn't seem to outrun to tear my house of belief to the ground, I ultimately could not deny that there is more than just the world we see with our physical eyes. I believe we are all spiritual creatures having a human experience, and we are all drawn in one way or another to seek and connect to that which is good. We want to know love. The journey of seeking begins in a place of darkness, of *not* knowing. In our pursuit of goodness and love, we encounter many false gods along the way that harm us and those around us. Good image, favor from authority, and being right were some of the false gods I worshipped. While they provided temporary satisfaction, I was always left empty and in pain. Yet I never stopped feeling the inescapable desire for *more than this*. With the rest of humanity, I continued to be drawn toward goodness—toward God. If that which is good is drawing humanity, I reasoned, then God indeed exists. It was the first brick laid in my reconstruction: I believe God is real!

I felt like I had a blank slate for God to fill up with His truth about Himself. I offered Him the opportunity to do so, and He did. I craved Scripture like a newborn needs their mother's milk. I examined what the Christian faith, with all its divisions and shades of doctrines, says about God and salvation. I also craved an understanding of *other* religions. This was new, since before my deconstruction I avoided other religions' texts like poison. This relentless search for the truth had poked major holes in my fear. So many of my core beliefs proved to be lies. I saw Freedom Village's legalism—the strict adherence to rule-following to earn salvation—for what it really was. I felt my old self fading away and hope filling up the new me. I spent hours underlining and considering Scripture about the Holy Spirit. The apostle Paul's radical letters in the New Testament about being adopted into God's family as children jumped off the page at me. This God, the one revealed in Christ, is freely inviting *all* people? In *this* God's perspective, there is no division among Greeks and Jews, the enslaved and the free, male and female...we are all *the same* to Him? If our source were to look, act, talk, teach, and love like Jesus Christ, that would be very good news. And there it was, written in Scripture. Not only did I know that God was real, I knew God was *good*.

I was finally experiencing the faith I had assumed I had my whole life. It was like thinking I knew what parenthood was versus the deep, personal understanding of unconditional love I had once I actually had kids. Knowledge is nothing compared to understanding, and understanding requires experience. I was awakening, and every day felt like good news.

God loved me. I was loved. That was my first and most important identity. The more I started living from that place, the less afraid I became. The constant anxiety that had kept me safe at Freedom Village disappeared. I had no idea it could feel so good to not be afraid of God. I knew who my Father was. I had found my true identity, and it was a game-changer.

Don't misunderstand me: I'm still susceptible to fear. I keep discovering new ways that fear connects to my life. There's no erasing the past and the trauma that shaped me. But I've found that God doesn't need to erase our past; He embraces it. I feel like John Nash in the movie *A Beautiful Mind*, when he accepts that he will always see people who aren't there but that he can resist them. Fear will always walk with me, but it isn't *a part of me* anymore because I'm connected to the source of love and truth. I trust that God's plan for me is good and know His will is that I'm never spiritually lost again.

In Matthew 7, Jesus tells a parable about the wisdom of building a house upon a rock. It goes something like this: A foolish man builds his house upon the sand. When the wind and rain come, it's all destroyed. A wise man builds his house upon the rock. When the wind and rain come, it stands firm. When I was a child, I understood this parable to mean that I needed to build my life on Christ, the rock. If I built my life on sand, which was anything that isn't Christ, I would be completely destroyed.

At Freedom Village, I tried my best to keep Christ at the center of my life, but all of my best efforts were like building on the sand. My fear-based obedience was building on the sand. My good works were building on the sand. My adherence to the rules was building on the sand. When the storm of my deconstruction washed the sand away, I was not destroyed, because of the bedrock *beneath* the sand.

Humans are often foolish. We tend to build things on sand. I made a mistake building my life upon Pastor's warped view of God. But grace—the reality that we are one with God through the revelation of Christ Jesus—can often be found only at rock bottom. Grace is the bedrock beneath us all. And it turns out that rock bottom is a pretty firm foundation to build from. The more I know how it feels to stand on the firm foundation of the grace of God, the less I end up building my beliefs on changing sands. Whenever I do start building on lies again, another storm always blows through to wash away everything but the truth of grace in Christ. It feels like I'm grounded on steady rock.

I learned that all the work I'd done to supposedly put God at the center of my life at Freedom Village and in the years afterward was building on sand. I couldn't love God more by *trying* to love

God more. I could only love Him to the degree that I believed He loved *me*. The only effort I needed to make as a Christian was to remember who I was in Christ. I was already made whole in Christ, and that identity is the gift God gave us to get through this life.

Oddly enough, coming to this understanding of who I was felt like discovering something for the first time as much as it felt like remembering something I had long forgotten. I think I finally believed the one thing I had always hoped was true. Knowing who I was opened the windows and doors of my heart, and it flushed out every bit of fear. That scared little girl who always felt unworthy and disappointing was gone.

As I rebuilt the tenets of my faith from an uncorrupted foundation, I became a true disciple. I can finally learn directly from God rather than through an intermediary. I can understand my fallen nature and my unworthiness without shame. I'm one more person who can see clearly, one less person walking unseeing through the darkness. In this world, it can seem as if evil is burning our souls to ashes, but God makes beauty from those ashes. God is not threatened by evil. This is the God of death and *then* life, where grace always wins. My experiences at Freedom Village harmed me immeasurably, but I've prospered in spite of it—perhaps because of it. What a story God can write.

Certain lies have taken a very long time to unbelieve. Spiritual fear had its way with my mind for so long; the muscle memory remains. The game-changer, though, is the awareness that when I am afraid or scared of God, I am not seeing who He is. That is good news when you've lived believing that closeness with God should result in fear of Him. The frightened girl of my youth is slowly being replaced by a woman who knows exactly who she is. I don't have to prove anything to anyone. The difference I feel is Christ in me, now able to move freely and help me learn.

After such an intense process of deconstructing and reconstructing my faith anew, most of my old beliefs were behind me, though I began to feel like an outsider in certain Christian circles. I wasn't sure where I belonged as it related to the corporate church or communities of faith, but I knew who my Father was and I knew who I was. I was born again. Now, to live.

15

FREEDOM

NEARLY THIRTEEN YEARS after I left Freedom Village, I drove back to the campus. I still live only a few miles away, but my usual driving routes don't happen to take me past it often.

The sign out front announcing "Freedom Village USA: North America's Premier Home for Troubled Teens" had been taken down. Freedom Village shut its doors in 2019, after media reports and grassroots efforts prevented Pastor from expanding to another state.

As I drove down the long, tree-lined driveway, there was no indication of what this place once was. There were no flags out front, no bleachers or scoreboards on the expansive front lawn. There were no security officers in the shed next to the welcome sign that read "Don't even think about smoking on this property!"

Going back there was like returning to my hometown to find it abandoned. It was eerie. The ministry was at one time a massive entity. This campus had been full of teens doing chores, cooking in the cafeteria, attending school in the classrooms, practicing sports on the field and basketball courts, singing at choir practice, tending horses in the barn. It had been so alive, and now it was lifeless.

When I was a child, I took pride in my conviction that if Freedom Village were ever to shut down, my family would be the last to leave, and even then, we would follow Pastor wherever he went. I've only recently started to realize how odd it was that I never considered leaving without Pastor until I was twenty-four years old. I still don't believe I would have left Freedom Village had my family and friends not gone first.

Once I left, I so desperately wanted to step into a new life that I tried to put Freedom Village as far out of my mind as I could. I had hoped my ghosts would stay in the past, tied to this Lakemont property like the ghosts of storybooks are tied to the houses they haunt.

I'm one of those people who spends a lot of time and energy in my head, lost in my own thoughts. Given that I trust that God is real, I don't know why I wouldn't naturally spend a lot of time thinking about ways to connect with the source of all that is good. But just as bad things happen to everyone everywhere, something bad happened to me at Freedom Village. I experienced consistent, severe abuse of my mind, the place where I inherently spend a lot of time. Pastor, the man who ruled by fear and shaped my earliest understanding of God, did the most damage there. This man took my pure, innocent belief and turned it into a poison that caused me years of suffering. The God I knew then was like Pastor.

By the time I was a teenager, my mind was Hell. I was terrified of the God I could never stop loving. Anxiety ruled my life. I spent massive amounts of energy performing, both on stage and off, convincing myself and everyone else that I was fine. And leaving Freedom Village didn't just flip that switch off. I left full-time ministry. I held it together as best I could while I had children. It was then that my severe lack of understanding about the love of

God began to manifest. I had always performed so hard to earn God's favor, but as a young mother living apart from a caring community, I was too tired to perform. I couldn't shake the guilt and constant fear that plagued me, as I had been spiritually conditioned to associate failure with punishment.

Freedom Village was my Hell on Earth, but that place was just the beginning of this story. Reconnecting with the pure belief in God that my parents had fostered in me healed fear's damage in my mind. Love, even when I didn't understand it, saved me from a very real, very *now*, Hell. And waiting for me were big, wide-open fields of grace. Heaven is the reality that I am loved exactly as I am. I don't have to perform. I don't have to try to please people. Being right or wrong doesn't change my value. Hell is all fear. Heaven is all love. I have known both.

ALL TOO MANY of the people I've talked to who have come through the doors of Freedom Village say they wish they could move on and forget about it, but they can't. We can't. Maybe our ghosts didn't follow us out from the inside—maybe we never actually left Freedom Village in our minds, even as we physically walked away. Many of us are still there in the ways we perceive our world. Pastor's voice narrated my thoughts for years after I left, hurling accusations at myself about the ways I didn't measure up. I responded to pressure, rules, and authority exactly the way I had at Freedom Village. Others I've talked to moved on to churches in the real world with the same atmosphere of spiritual fear and control that existed at Freedom Village. They still haven't *left*.

It's often hard to have conversations about this ministry. Many who were there have said, "That place was Hell." Those who are sure that Freedom Village was a cult tend to get upset when someone else suggests it was a ministry where people received help. A number of people have said, "God was in that place." Those who are certain God was in the midst of Freedom Village tend to get upset when someone suggests that it was Hell. Regardless of which side someone is on, most people who passed through there seem to want to just put it behind them and move on, me included.

But when I decided to document my story, I began asking God, "What happened at Freedom Village?" I wanted to go back in time and see it for what it was so I could tell the story properly and truthfully. And as I allowed myself to remember, I clearly saw the disorder, oppression, fear, control, and wickedness. It *was* Hell. Pastor hadn't been a messenger of God. He was just a man who wanted to be relevant and who used people to make his own dreams happen. He didn't know the truth any more than I did; he was a slave to fear the entire time.

I was afraid that if I told the truth about the spiritual abuse we endured, I would be betraying God. So, accepting that Freedom Village was a dark place, I grieved all that happened there and all that did not. I grieved for the people who bear scars that will last a lifetime. From my grief, another question formed, an accusation: "God, where were You?" I followed it with the desperate plea, "Please, show it to me through Your eyes."

And that's when I *actually* left Freedom Village; I left after leaving. I looked again with clear eyes and saw beautiful lifelong connections, faith, service, and goodwill. Freedom Village was still Hell, but God was there. *It was Hell, and God was there!*

There was so much wrongdoing, and God worked, moved, and loved us in the midst of it all, completely unthreatened by the harm that was being done in His name and intent on making all things new.

My willingness to open my eyes and look at the experiences

that haunted me allowed God to flood my mind with light and clarity. I'm not avoiding Freedom Village, because I'm not afraid of it anymore. The ghosts of that place are nothing but shadows that must vanish when the light shines on it.

I know more now about what Freedom Village was, and it still isn't simple or easy to explain. It was many things. It was a cult, a church, a rehabilitation center, a prison, a launchpad, a place of healing, and a place of abuse. It was the result of a man using God's name to make money off a vulnerable group of people: concerned parents and their children, along with the well-meaning Christians who supported the ministry. Freedom Village gave Pastor unquestioned power through a system that punished and threatened people into submission for the sake of behavioral change. It was an empire, and I watched both its rise and its fall.

I'm willing to risk appearing like a disgruntled, misguided naysayer if that means I can effectively shine a light on something truly dark. I'm also willing to risk appearing like an out-of-touch Christian who ignores evil and calls it faith. Because it's not black or white: Freedom Village was Hell, *and* God was there.

Those who close their eyes are captive to darkness—not because evil has any true power but because they have shut their eyes. Those who refuse to see the evils of Freedom Village continue to be haunted by it, and those who refuse to see that God was there are unable to move on.

AS I WORKED through my story and my faith on my blog, *Out from the Inside*, many people found a lot to disagree with me about, sometimes to my face and sometimes behind my back. I understand that. I've thought a lot about how I have become the type of Christian who used to scare the old Christian me.

I've also changed my mind about how often I need to defend myself. It seems like a waste of time when I'm busy wandering these fields of grace. It feels unbelievably right to give myself grace. It feels even better to experience giving other people grace. In Hell, fear told me that using grace was to risk abusing it. Looking back, I can't believe I lived like that. Understanding grace has been changing my life. Fear has no choice but to leave me alone. I don't feel guilty anymore either. Without guilt, I can do whatever I want, because grace has changed what I want: to know the love of God.

I've seen the undeniable power of God's love; it saved me from Hell. There's no way I'm ever going back there. Old wounds still need healing, and I have much more to learn about the God of grace. Nothing seems too hard for Him, though, so I'm optimistic. Since deconstructing and rebuilding my faith, I've felt the promise of 1 John 4:18 in real time: I am being perfected by God. It fulfills Jesus's ultimate promise: "I am making everything new." I've declared freedom from fear, and God's love continues to work on me. Had I stayed captive to fear, I would have been afraid to share the truth. I would have kept everyone at arm's length for the rest of my life. I would never have stepped foot in a church again.

But I was born a seeker, and my mind longs for truth. In my bleakest wanderings, I begged to know truth, and it guided me out of the darkness like a string of lights. At my slow and fearful pace, I followed my guide through the unlearning of lies. When light shines on a lie, it is revealed; I no longer believe it, now that I can see how I hurt myself by believing it. Each time truth demolishes another lie, I can move forward with less fear. The process is gradual, but I'm moving faster lately. Love is casting fear out of my mind and off my eyes, and the light shines brighter and brighter. This is my salvation story.

In practical terms, this process means that I'm more reverent toward and less afraid of God than ever before. I've discovered a love, tolerance, and patience toward my body and mind like I've never known. I'm starting to love myself! And it doesn't end there. Love extends into my world, to my friends and to those I've called my enemies. It turns out that forgiving does not lead to freedom; it's the other way around. Believing the truth about myself has opened up a radical freedom, creating true forgiveness in my heart for myself, for those who hurt me at Freedom Village, and for Pastor.

Today, I want Pastor to know the mercy and grace of the God of love, which is the only thing that can save him. I still hope he can see clearly what he has done, know the horror he unleashed, and fully understand the harm he has caused. When he stands accountable for it all, perhaps he can finally see Jesus as the reconciliation with God. Pastor is forgiven. I hope he can know it.

There is something else I've been given that I never asked God for because, after Freedom Village, I flat-out didn't want it: community. Mike, the kids, and I began visiting a local church in 2013, mostly because I thought it was good for our kids to attend church. Shortly after we started attending, Mike began to play guitar on the church's worship team. I was perfectly content to hide my talents, to hide myself. I didn't want to be used, and I didn't want to know anyone. I never even called it "our church." I called it "the church we go to."

Years passed this way before I began deconstruction. As that process unfolded, I realized that though I had always performed, I still had so much I wanted to learn about worship. The ballet classes I taught at my mom's studio conflicted with worship rehearsals, so I didn't make any moves to audition for the worship team at the church we went to. But my desire to sing continued to grow until I realized I didn't need to be on the worship team to worship. I had the freedom to sing wherever and whenever I wanted. I began to sing in worship at home while I was cleaning the house, or in the car driving to and from work. Anytime I was alone, I was singing and experiencing profound worship. It was steadfast; it required no one but me and God. I developed such a passion for singing in worship that when the opportunity arose for me to join the church's worship team in 2019, I felt completely free to do it. Instead of a performance, leading worship on Sunday mornings was an extension of my private worship with God.

Don't mistake this step into community as a sign that I was ready to truly connect. Even as I joined the worship team, my plan was to sing at church but keep everyone at arm's length. I was there to sing and worship God—I didn't need friends. I didn't *want* friends, at least not ones who were church people. My mistrust of the church understandably ran deep. And yet, I've been consistently drawn into this church and a group of people who've loved me well, despite my baggage. I found myself trusting: first God, then myself, and finally other people.

It started with just one church friend, Tracey. Our profoundly beautiful friendship has ushered in an understanding of church as a space where it is possible for people to love one another freely. That type of love changes our minds. My mind changed yet again because I found love in the place I was least willing to look for it: a church. My friendships there are truly a miracle, and they're the reason I eventually began to call this community "my church."

But God took my growth a step further: In 2023, I left my job at a café to work at my church full-time on the creative arts team and in children's ministry. Working with children in the realm of spirituality is healing parts of my heart that I lost hope for somewhere along the way. Every time I lead worship on Sunday mornings, I am in wonder at the miracles I've experienced in my mind and heart.

I didn't ask for this gift, yet here it is. Let me be clear: the gift isn't my church, which is as wonderful and flawed as any church is. The gift is my healing. I can be anywhere and find the glory of God. I am not afraid. I love all people. God is making all things new, and it's all His work, not mine. I am at rest. This is Heaven on Earth, here and now. If God had told me all of this would ensue when I left Freedom Village, I simply wouldn't have believed Him.

This is true freedom.

A NOTE FROM THE AUTHOR

AFTER I LEFT FREEDOM VILLAGE, I was surprised at how unbelievable my story is to many people. I was also surprised to find out how common the theological framework I grew up with is in mainstream Christian culture.

Whether you're Baptist or Pentecostal, Catholic or Protestant, Wesleyan or Calvinist, mixing fear into faith makes it downright poisonous to consume. I pray that my story can reach those who have been living in spiritual fear, whether instilled in you by a pastor or a family member, and that you will find hope in my healing. It's possible to be wrong about everything—and for that to be good news.

Sometimes, readers on my blog ask me to share my belief system with them, to tell them what's spiritually true. Oftentimes, I am being asked to choose a side, to pick a camp. I can't and I won't. Forcing religion on others, especially those who are spiritually hungry, is what caused my suffering in the first place. I don't know it all, but I know my story and what I've been through, and I'm finally beginning to see the beauty God wants to make of that.

Too many people have been burned by the humans in charge of church and religion. I'm one of them. But I am not walking away from my faith; rather, I am running toward truth with more confidence and abandon than I ever have.

If you've been burned, you are not alone. "Everyone will be salted with fire," the Gospel of Mark assures us. If our God is a consuming fire, then the fire is God's love itself, burning away everything that doesn't belong until only the true you is left. Everyone must be baptized with fire.

If that sentence puts fear or dread into your heart, then you need to know this truth: the Refiner's fire is love. It cleanses us from all unrighteousness. It removes that which hurts us, the children of God. Some of us have been burned by abusive relationships or our environments. Some have been burned by the pursuit of wealth or fame. Others have been burned by fear-based religious systems. I promise that whatever it is that has nearly ruined you up until this point won't have the final say. Death is not an ending; I know because I have spiritually died and come back from the dead to tell you all this: The very thing that hurt you is the place you must return to in order to find healing. Do not be afraid. You do not walk alone. God and His love are more real and infinitely better than you've ever thought they could be. Dare to believe it with me.

—Mary Rosenberger

A NOTE FROM THE PUBLISHER

ONE OF THE things I find most beautiful about Mary's story is that Pastor no longer holds power over her. It's not relevant how Freedom Village fell apart or where Pastor ended up. What matters is that Mary has found grace, that grace extends to Pastor, and she has forgiven him.

I love this resolution for Mary and for her story. Yet as a journalist, I long to know more. If you're among the curious readers with lingering questions about Pastor and Freedom Village, I have some answers for you.

THE EXODUS of so many staff members in 2011, including Mary and her family, shook the foundations of Freedom Village. Some of the staff who left filed a lawsuit for unpaid wages—and they won. Between the back pay, interest, and penalties, Freedom Village owed more than one and a half million dollars. Not for the first time, Freedom Village filed for bankruptcy. This time, however, the bankruptcy court denied the request, leaving Freedom Village responsible for its financial obligations.

Over the next several years, Freedom Village's debts lingered. Creditors on his tail, Pastor sold Freedom Village's campus and other property for a little over a million dollars in 2019. He made plans to relocate the ministry to a remote area of the Blue Ridge Mountains and rebrand as Victory Village USA. When South Carolina's paper of record reported on Pastor's plans—along with Freedom Village's history of legal, financial, and spiritual program woes—former Freedom Village program students mobilized against Victory Village. The organization that had planned to partner with Freedom Village to enable the move distanced itself from Pastor. Within four months, the relocation to South Carolina was scrapped. Freedom Village fizzled into nonexistence.

The 2019 New York Child Victims Act created additional pressure for Pastor in 2020. The law extended the statute of limitations for survivors of child sexual abuse to file lawsuits against individuals or organizations. This spurred a pair of lawsuits against Pastor and Freedom Village USA. Both cases were settled out of court as their respective trial dates loomed, nearly four years after they were filed.

Citing liberal hatred in New York, Pastor left the Finger Lakes region behind and moved to Florida, then to Mississippi. In 2020, the IRS granted nonprofit status to new "ministries" Pastor named after himself. As a 501(c)(3), his organization is free from federal income tax and can receive tax-deductible gifts. According to IRS tax filings, the nonprofit collected nearly half a million dollars in grants and contributions in its first two years of operation. Pastor's website asserts that donations support his radio and podcast programs; a fund for Pastor's consulting work with youth homes;

Operation Mercy, which bolstered the now-defunct Freedom Village Ukraine; and financial support for Pastor and his family's missionary work. Pastor teased plans for Freedom Village Dominican Republic in 2022, though they were later abandoned.

Pastor continues to solicit donations today.

—Alysha Love

BOOK CLUB QUESTIONS

1. Mary dedicates *Freedom Village* to her parents. How is this consistent with her message of grace and love?
2. What do you think most resonated with Mary about the biblical passage from the book of Habakkuk? ("How long, Lord, must I call for help, but you do not listen?")
3. How might the rules of Freedom Village have created an environment conducive to abuse? How might the rules have created structure for good?
4. Freedom Village was a unique environment, but Mary's experiences aren't uncommon. How do Mary's viewpoints, experiences, or resulting behaviors resonate with you? What situations in your past align on some level with hers?
5. How honest do you think Mary has been about her experiences inside Freedom Village? Is she a reliable narrator? What evidence supports your conclusion?

BOOK CLUB QUESTIONS

6. How did you feel when Mary and her extended family left Freedom Village? How come?
7. How did Mary's deconstruction of her beliefs affect you personally? What do you think it would be like for you to go through a similar process, if you haven't already?
8. How does it change your perspective if you were to consider Freedom Village in grayscale, rather than black-or-white thinking?
9. If you could ask Mary anything after reading her memoir, what would it be?
10. What message or messages did you take away from *Freedom Village*?

RESOURCES FOR READERS

Mental Health Resources

Crisis Text Line
　　Text HOME to 741741
　　https://crisistextline.org

988 Suicide and Crisis Lifeline
　　Call or text 988
　　https://988lifeline.org

Mental Health America
　　https://mhanational.org

National Alliance on Mental Illness
　　https://nami.org

National Institute of Mental Health
　　https://nimh.nih.gov

RESOURCES FOR READERS

To Write Love on Her Arms
https://twloha.com

National Alliance for Eating Disorders Helpline
Call (866) 662-1235
https://allianceforeatingdisorders.com

National Eating Disorders Association
https://nationaleatingdisorders.org

Eating Disorder Hope
https://eatingdisorderhope.com

Postpartum Support International
https://postpartum.net

Psychology Today, to find a therapist
https://psychologytoday.com/us/therapists

Abuse Resources

We Warned Them Campaign
https://wewarnedthem.org

Breaking Code Silence
https://breakingcodesilence.org

Alliance Against Seclusion & Restraint
https://endseclusion.org

Religious Trauma Institute
https://religioustraumainstitute.com

RESOURCES FOR READERS

National Domestic Violence Hotline, for mental, spiritual, sexual, and physical abuse
Call (800) 799-7233
Text BEGIN to 88788
https://thehotline.org

Rape, Abuse & Incest National Network
Call (800) 656-4673
https://rainn.org

Education, Work, and Financial Resources

Earn a GED® high school equivalency diploma
https://ged.com

Cara Collective, for free workforce training
https://caracollective.org

Jobs for the Future
https://jff.org

US FDIC's How Money Smart Are You?
https://www.playmoneysmart.fdic.gov

Operation Hope, for free financial literacy coaching
https://operationhope.org

Money Management International
https://moneymanagement.org

US government benefit programs
https://usa.gov/benefits

RESOURCES FOR READERS

Find Help, for free or reduced-cost local food, housing, healthcare, and financial resources
https://findhelp.org

Christian Faith Resources

The Gospels of the Bible

Mere Christianity **by C. S. Lewis**

Out from the Inside
https://wearetheoutsiders.com

ACKNOWLEDGMENTS

To the man who has chosen to walk with me since I was fourteen:
   Mike, thank you. This journey has been wild, yet you have never wanted out. You have been my steadfast and loyal companion through all that we have gone through, and I know how rare that is. You have seen me as I am and you're not going anywhere. You have loved me in all of my forms. I know I am yours. You have given grace as I grow and change and become a more whole version of myself. My healing is for more than just me…it's ours, too. Our story is my favorite one in the big-picture story of my life. You are everything to me! Thank you for walking with me and standing by me. I love you. I have all I need. I choose you, forever. Every step, together.

To my children, Leah, Noah, and Claire:
   The process of motherhood has taught me more about myself than any book, class, or therapist ever could. I don't think my mind would have begun to think for itself without someone else to protect and consider. God used me being your mom to save my life. Every day of raising you, getting to know you, and loving you has done the impossible for me…it has taught me that unconditional love is real. I didn't and couldn't know that before you all came along. I love being your mom. Thank you for being exactly who you are. You will grow and change because that's what people do, and I will love every version of you along the way.

To my mom and dad, Cheryl and Rich:

Mom, you have given me so many gifts. You gave me a love for music and art. I would be so lost without them! You have taught me how to make so much of very little. I watched you take troubled teenagers and create choirs, ensembles, small groups, trios, and soloists who could sing with such conviction and skill that it left people in awe, forever changed. Your ability to create and inspire is the heart of God on display! Thank you for every lesson, every sacrifice you made, and every moment of loving me for exactly who I am. We are more than mom and daughter. We are sisters and friends. I love you so much!

Dad, the ultimate storyteller. Every time you created a story or relived a profound movie scene with tears in your eyes, you instilled a deep appreciation in me for well-told stories. I experience life in metaphors because of you. Your belief in supernatural, mystical things like spiritual warfare are the roots of my faith. Your utter lack of fear regarding evil was passed along to me and is what gave me the courage to write this book. Thank you for always reminding me of the only answer...seek first the kingdom. I love you, Dad.

To my big sister, Sarah, and my big brother, Jesse:

Sarah, you have taught me so much in my life, from the ability to hear harmonies to confidence and belief in my own worth as a singer. You have been such a part of my musical life! I also watched you lean into faith through many dark seasons of life at Freedom Village and beyond into the real world. I wouldn't be who I am today without watching and learning from my big sister.

Jesse, sometimes I wish I had been able to question and resist the controlling atmosphere at Freedom Village like you did. I now admire the very thing I used to fear about you. Your beautiful mind led you to the outside sooner than the rest of us, and I am so proud of you for following it. It showed me that the grace of God exists far beyond the boundaries we place on Him out of fear. I love you for that. Never stop wandering and exploring.

To my friends, the people who make up my world and inspire me to seek truth, speak truth, and live free:

To the staff kids at Freedom Village, I treasure these relationships so deeply. Sarah, Becky, Vicky, Richard, Sarah, Jaci, Kaiti, and so many more...we were family. Nobody has a story quite like ours, and there is so much beauty in that. Every time I hear from a staff kid, it heals my heart even more. I pray that my words will create space for us all to reflect, acknowledge the good and the bad, and move on. We were the only group of people at Freedom Village who didn't choose to be there, but we can choose to leave, even after all these years. I am here with you to listen, speak, and share. I love you all!

Tracey, when I told God that I would go back to church but not love anyone in it, I can't imagine the delight He had when we finally met in 2020! Our friendship is a revelation of the heart of God, and this book would not have been written without a friend like you who is fearless in the pursuit of truth and healing. Thank you for everything. We get to live like this!

Jecca, from the moment I met you, you have inspired me to be myself. Your authentic beauty has always invited me into a deeper way of living. I am so grateful for our friendship and mutual openness to learn about God and ourselves. Your genuine support and belief in me as I tell this story means so much. I love you!

Fellow artists from Seneca School of Performing Arts who allowed me to create art for and with them, I will never forget those years! I wouldn't be the storyteller and artist I am today without the years of creating with you. What a time we had!

Coworkers and friends from Oak Hill Café, your reactions to

my life story inspired the creation of the blog. Every one of you is a part of this story, because without you asking about it, I wouldn't have felt the need to go back to Freedom Village in my mind. Your curiosity and support taught me to talk about it. Thank you for listening to my rants during my faith deconstruction as I peeled potatoes and questioned the foundations of Christianity. You all could have seriously rolled your eyes and ignored me! It was my connection to the café that eventually led to my incredible editor and publisher.

Alysha Love and Payette Publishing, words cannot describe my appreciation and thanks for how you have handled my story. From the moment I first spoke with you, I knew I trusted you. Thank you for caring about me and how I needed to tell this story. Your gifts and support are exactly what I have needed to make this happen!

Barbie Halaby at Monocle Editing, I am so grateful to have had your keen eye on the manuscript of this book! You truly have a gift. For every read-through, reread, edit, and micro-edit, I sincerely thank you.

My current coworkers and friends in the church, I wouldn't have believed God, even if He told me about you all. I didn't know trust was possible again. Thank you for welcoming me as I am. The relationships I made as a result of that place have healed parts of my heart that I didn't even know were hurt, let alone knew to ask for healing in. I think I can say in honesty now that I love the church. It is a miracle. I wouldn't have written this book without this healing. It has not been easy, but it has all been good.

ABOUT THE AUTHOR

Mary Rosenberger is the author of the blog *Out from the Inside*, where she first documented her upbringing in a religious cult—and her eventual escape from its grasp. *Freedom Village: A Memoir* is Mary's first book.

Mary continues to write about her unending pursuit of the heart of God on her blog. She explores her lifelong passions for singing and dance at her church, which is decidedly *not* a cult. Mary lives in upstate New York with her husband, three children, and a veritable menagerie of pets.

Milton Keynes UK
Ingram Content Group UK Ltd.
UKHW022330271124
451619UK00018B/131/J